The Supporters' Guide

to

Non-League Football

2008

GW00481881

EDITOR
John Robinson

Sixteenth Edition

For details of our range of almost 1,400 books and 300 DVDs, visit our web site or contact us using the information shown below.

British Library Cataloguing in Publication Data
A catalogue record for this book is available from the British Library

ISBN: 978-1-86223-159-7

Manufactured in the UK by LPPS Ltd, Wellingborough, NN8 3PJ

FOREWORD

Our thanks go to the numerous club officials who have aided us in the compilation of information contained in this guide and also to Michael Robinson (page layouts), Bob Budd (cover artwork) and Tony Brown (Cup Statistics – www.soccerdata.com) for the part they have played.

Where we use the term 'Child' for concessionary prices, this is often also the price charged to Senior Citizens.

Following the latest reorganisation of the Non-League Pyramid structure, we have confined this guide to the 68 Football Conference Clubs in Steps 1 & 2.

In a year which saw the demise of several senior clubs and the enforced amalgamation of others, we can only hope that the forthcoming season will bring less disruption and financial hardship and more stability for clubs in Steps 1 & 2 of the Pyramid!

Finally, we would like to wish our readers a safe and happy spectating season.

John Robinson
EDITOR

CONTENTS

THE FOOTBALL CONFERENCE BLUE SQUARE NATIONAL

Address   Riverside House, 14B High Street, Crayford, Kent   DA1 4HG

Phone (01322) 411021   **Fax** (01322) 411022

Web site   www.footballconference.co.uk

Clubs for the 2007/2008 Season

ALDERSHOT TOWN FC

Founded: 1992
Former Names: Aldershot FC
Nickname: 'Shots'
Ground: Recreation Ground, High Street, Aldershot, GU11 1TW
Record Attendance: 7,500 (18/11/2000)
Pitch Size: 117 × 76 yards

Colours: Red shirts with Blue trim, Red shorts
Telephone Nº: (01252) 320211
Fax Number: (01252) 324347
Club Secretary: (01252) 320211– Graham Hortop
Ground Capacity: 7,500
Seating Capacity: 1,832
Web site: www.theshots.co.uk

GENERAL INFORMATION
Supporters Club: c/o Club
Telephone Nº: (01252) 320211
Car Parking: Municipal Car Park is adjacent
Coach Parking: Contact the club for information
Nearest Railway Station: Aldershot (5 mins. walk)
Nearest Bus Station: Aldershot (5 minutes walk)
Club Shop: At the ground
Opening Times: Matchdays only
Telephone Nº: (01252) 320211
Police Telephone Nº: (01252) 324545

GROUND INFORMATION
Away Supporters' Entrances & Sections:
Accommodation in the East Bank Terrace, Bill Warren section (South Stand)

ADMISSION INFO (2007/2008 PRICES)
Adult Standing: £13.00
Adult Seating: £16.00
Child Standing: £9.00
Child Seating: £9.00
Senior Citizen Standing: £9.00
Senior Citizen Seating: £10.00
Programme Price: £2.50

DISABLED INFORMATION
Wheelchairs: Accommodated in a covered area
Helpers: Admitted
Prices: Free for the disabled. Helpers charged £5.00
Disabled Toilets: Available
Contact: (01252) 320211   (Bookings are necessary)

Travelling Supporters' Information:
Routes: From the M3: Exit at Junction 4 and follow signs for Aldershot (A331). Leave the A331 at the A323 exit (Ash Road) and continue along into the High Street. The ground is just past the Railway Bridge on the right; From the A31: Continue along the A31 to the junction with the A331, then as above; From the A325 (Farnborough Road): Follow signs to the A323 then turn left into Wellington Avenue. The ground is just off the 2nd roundabout on the left – the floodlights are clearly visible.

ALTRINCHAM FC

Founded: 1903
Former Names: None
Nickname: 'The Robins'
Ground: Moss Lane, Altrincham   WA15 8AP
Record Attendance: 10,275 (February 1925)
Pitch Size: 110 × 74 yards

Colours: Red and White striped shirts, Black shorts
Telephone Nº: (0161) 928-1045
Daytime Phone Nº: (0161) 928-1045
Fax Number: (0161) 926-9934
Ground Capacity: 6,085
Seating Capacity: 1,154
Web site: www.altrinchamfc.com

GENERAL INFORMATION

Supporters Trust: Paul Daine, STAR, c/o Club
Telephone Nº: –
Car Parking: Adjacent to the ground
Coach Parking: By Police Direction
Nearest Railway Station: Altrincham (5 minutes walk)
Nearest Bus Station: Altrincham
Club Shop: At the ground
Opening Times: 9.00am – 5.00pm Matchdays & Weekdays
Telephone Nº: (0161) 928-1045
Police Telephone Nº: (0161) 872-5050

GROUND INFORMATION

Away Supporters' Entrances & Sections:
Richmans End turnstiles and accommodation

ADMISSION INFO (2007/2008 PRICES)

Adult Standing: £12.00
Adult Seating: £14.00
Concessionary Standing: £7.00
Concessionary Seating: £8.00
Under-11s: £2.00
Programme Price: £2.00

DISABLED INFORMATION

Wheelchairs: 3 spaces are available each for home and away fans adjacent to the Away dugout
Helpers: Admitted
Prices: Free for the disabled. £12.00 for helpers
Disabled Toilets: Yes
Contact: (0161) 928-1045   (Bookings are necessary)

Travelling Supporters' Information:
Routes: Exit the M56 at either Junction 6 or 7 and following the signs Altrincham FC.

BURTON ALBION FC

Founded: 1950
Former Names: None
Nickname: 'The Brewers'
Ground: The Pirelli Stadium, Princess Way, Burton-on-Trent DE13 0AR
Record Attendance: 6,000 (8th January 2006)
Pitch Size: 110 × 72 yards

Colours: Shirts are Yellow with Black trim, shorts are Black with Yellow Trim
Telephone Nº: (01283) 565938
Fax Number: (01283) 523199
Ground Capacity: 6,000
Seating Capacity: 2,000
Web site: www.burtonalbionfc.co.uk

GENERAL INFORMATION

Supporters Club: c/o Club
Telephone Nº: (01283) 565938
Car Parking: Available at the ground
Coach Parking: Rykneld Trading Estate, Derby Road
Nearest Railway Station: Burton-on-Trent (1½ miles)
Nearest Bus Station: Burton-on-Trent (1½ miles)
Club Shop: At the ground
Opening Times: Weekdays 9.00am – 5.00pm and Matchdays from 1½ hours before kick-off
Telephone Nº: (01283) 565938
Police Telephone Nº: 08543 302010

GROUND INFORMATION

Away Supporters' Entrances & Sections:
East Stand, Derby Road

ADMISSION INFO (2007/2008 PRICES)

Adult Standing: £12.00
Adult Seating: £14.00
Child Standing: £3.00
Child Seating: £5.00
Senior Citizen Standing: £10.00
Senior Citizen Seating: £12.00
Programme Price: £2.50

DISABLED INFORMATION

Wheelchairs: Over 78 spaces available for home and away fans in the designated disabled areas
Helpers: Admitted
Prices: Normal prices for the disabled. Free for helpers
Disabled Toilets: Available in all stands
Contact: (01283) 565938 (Bookings are necessary)

Travelling Supporters' Information:
Routes: From the M1, North and South: Exit at Junction 23A and join the A50 towards Derby (also signposted for Alton Towers). Join the A38 southbound at the Toyota factory (towards Burton & Lichfield) then exit for Burton North onto the A5121. Continue past the Pirelli factory on the right and the BP Garage and Cash & Carry on the left then turn into Princess Way at the roundabout; From the M5/6 South: Join the M42 northbound and exit onto the A446 signposted Lichfield. Follow signs for the A38 to Burton then exit onto A5121 as above; From the M6 North: Exit at Junction 15 and follow the A50 towards Stoke and Uttoxeter. Exit the A50 for the A38 southbound signposted Burton and Lichfield at the Toyota factory, then as above.

CAMBRIDGE UNITED FC

Founded: 1912
Former Name: Abbey United FC (1912-1951)
Nickname: 'U's' 'United'
Ground: Abbey Stadium, Newmarket Road,
Cambridge   CB5 8LN
Ground Capacity: 8,696
Seating Capacity: 4,376

Pitch Size: 110 × 72 yards
Record Attendance: 14,000 (1/5/70)
Colours: Amber shirts, Black shorts
Telephone Nº: (01223) 566500
Ticket Office: (01223) 566500
Fax Number: (01223) 566502
Web Site: www.cambridgeunited.com

GENERAL INFORMATION

Car Parking: Street parking only
Coach Parking: Coldhams Road
Nearest Railway Station: Cambridge (2 miles)
Nearest Bus Station: Cambridge City Centre
Club Shop: At the ground
Opening Times: Monday to Friday 9.00am to 5.00pm and
Matchdays 11.00am to kick-off
Telephone Nº: (01223) 566500
Police Telephone Nº: (01223) 358966

GROUND INFORMATION

Away Supporters' Entrances & Sections:
Coldham Common turnstiles 20-22 – Habbin Terrace (South)
and South Stand (Seating) turnstiles 23-26

ADMISSION INFO (2007/2008 PRICES)

Adult Standing: £12.00
Adult Seating: £15.00
Child Standing: £3.00
Child Seating: £3.00 (in the Family Stand) or £7.00
Concessionary Standing: £8.00
Concessionary Seating: £10.00
Programme Price: £2.50

DISABLED INFORMATION

Wheelchairs: 19 spaces in total for Home fans in the
disabled sections, in front of Main Stand and in the North
Terrace. 16 spaces for Away fans in the South Stand.
Helpers: One helper admitted per disabled fan
Prices: £8.00 for the disabled. Free of charge for helpers
Disabled Toilets: At the rear of the disabled section
Contact: (01223) 566500   (Bookings are necessary)

Travelling Supporters' Information: Routes: From the North: Take the A1 and A14 to Cambridge and then head towards Newmarket. Turn off onto the B1047, signposted for Cambridge Airport, Horningsea and Fen Ditton. Turn right at the top of the slip road and travel through Fen Ditton. Turn right at the traffic lights at the end of the village. Go straight on at the roundabout onto Newmarket Road. The ground is 500 yards on the left; From the South and East: Take the A10 or A130 to the M11. Head North to the A14. Then as from the North; From the West: Take the A422 to Cambridge and join the A14. Then as from North.
Bus Services: Services from the Railway Station to the City Centre and Nº 3 from the City Centre to the Ground.

CRAWLEY TOWN FC

Founded: 1896
Former Names: None
Nickname: 'Red Devils'
Ground: Broadfield Stadium, Brighton Road, Crawley, Sussex   RH11 9RX
Record Attendance: 4,516 (2004)
Pitch Size: 110 × 72 yards

Colours: Red shirts and shorts
Telephone N°: (01293) 410000 (Ground)
Daytime N°: (01293) 410000 (10.00am – 4.00pm)
Fax Number: (01293) 410002
Ground Capacity: 4,941
Seating Capacity: 1,150
Web site: www.crawleytownfc.net

GENERAL INFORMATION

Supporters Club: Alain Harper, 33 Nuthurst Close, Ifield, Crawley, Sussex
Telephone N°: (01293) 511764
Car Parking: 350 spaces available at the ground
Coach Parking: At the ground
Nearest Railway Station: Crawley (1 mile)
Nearest Bus Station: By the Railway Station
Club Shop: At the ground
Opening Times: Weekdays 10.00am to 4.00pm; Saturday matches 12.00pm to kick-off then one hour after the game; Mid-week matches 6.00pm to kick-off then one hour after the game
Telephone N°: (01293) 410000
Police Telephone N°: (08456) 070999

GROUND INFORMATION

Away Supporters' Entrances & Sections:
No usual segregation

ADMISSION INFO (2006/2007 PRICES)

Adult Standing: £12.00
Adult Seating: £15.00
Child Standing: £3.00
Child Seating: £5.00
Senior Citizen/Student Standing: £8.00
Senior Citizen/Student Seating: £10.00
Programme Price: £2.50

DISABLED INFORMATION

Wheelchairs: Accommodated in the disabled section of the Main Stand (Lift access available)
Helpers: One helper admitted per disabled fan
Prices: Normal prices apply
Disabled Toilets: Available
Contact: (01293) 410000   (Bookings are not necessary)

Travelling Supporters' Information:
Routes: Exit the M23 at Junction 11 and take the A23 towards Crawley. After ¼ mile, the Stadium is on the left. Take the first exit at the roundabout for the Stadium entrance.

DROYLSDEN FC

Founded: 1892
Former Names: None
Nickname: 'The Bloods'
Ground: Butchers Arms, Market Street, Droylsden, Manchester   M43 7AY
Record Attendance: 5,400 (1973)
Pitch Size: 110 × 70 yards

Colours: Red shirts with Black shorts
Telephone Nº: (0161) 370-1426
Daytime Phone Nº: (0161) 370-1426
Fax Number: (0161) 370-8341
Ground Capacity: 3,500
Seating Capacity: 500
Web site: www.droylsdenfc.co.uk

GENERAL INFORMATION

Supporters Club: c/o Club
Telephone Nº: –
Car Parking: Street parking only
Coach Parking: At the ground
Nearest Railway Station: Manchester Piccadilly
Nearest Bus Station: Ashton
Club Shop: At the ground
Opening Times: Matchdays only
Telephone Nº: (0161) 370-1426
Police Telephone Nº: (0161) 330-8321

GROUND INFORMATION

Away Supporters' Entrances & Sections:
No usual segregation

ADMISSION INFO (2007/2008 PRICES)

Adult Standing: £12.00
Adult Seating: £12.00
Concessionary Standing: £8.00
Concessionary Seating: £8.00
Note: Under-14s are admitted free of charge
Programme Price: £2.00

DISABLED INFORMATION

Wheelchairs: Accommodated beside the Stand
Helpers: Yes
Prices: Normal prices apply for the disabled and helpers
Disabled Toilets: Available
Contact: (0161) 370-1426   (Bookings are not necessary)

Travelling Supporters' Information:
Routes: Take the Manchester Outer Ring Road M60 and exit at Junction 23. Join the A635 towards Manchester and after the retail park on the left, take the centre lane, then turn right at the traffic lights onto the A662 signposted for Droylsden. At the next traffic lights, turn right onto Market Street and after 150 yards go straight on at the traffic lights. The entrance to the ground is 75 yards on the left.

EBBSFLEET UNITED FC

Founded: 1946
Former Names: Gravesend & Northfleet United FC, Gravesend United FC and Northfleet United FC
Nickname: 'The Fleet'
Ground: Stonebridge Road, Northfleet, Gravesend, Kent DA11 9GN
Record Attendance: 12,063 (1963)

Colours: Reds shirts with White shorts
Telephone Nº: (01474) 533796
Fax Number: (01474) 324754
Pitch Size: 112 × 72 yards
Ground Capacity: 5,258
Seating Capacity: 1,220
Web site: www.ebbsfleetunited.co.uk

GENERAL INFORMATION

Supporters Club: c/o Club
Telephone Nº: (01474) 533796
Car Parking: At the ground and also street parking
Coach Parking: At the ground
Nearest Railway Station: Northfleet (5 minutes walk)
Nearest Bus Station: Bus Stop outside the ground
Club Shop: At the ground
Opening Times: Matchdays only
Telephone Nº: (01474) 533796
Police Telephone Nº: (01474) 564346

GROUND INFORMATION

Away Supporters' Entrances & Sections:
Only some games are segregated – contact club for details

ADMISSION INFO (2006/2007 PRICES)

Adult Standing: £12.00
Adult Seating: £14.00
Senior Citizen/Child Standing: £6.00
Senior Citizen/Child Seating: £7.00
Programme Price: £2.50

DISABLED INFORMATION

Wheelchairs: 6 spaces are available in the Disabled Area in front of the Main Stand
Helpers: Admitted free of charge
Prices: Please phone the club for information
Disabled Toilets: Available in the Main Stand
Contact: (01474) 533796 (Bookings are necessary)

Travelling Supporters' Information:
Routes: Take the A2 to the Northfleet/Southfleet exit and follow signs for Northfleet (B262). Go straight on at the first roundabout then take the 2nd exit at the 2nd roundabout into Thames Way and follow the football signs for the ground.

EXETER CITY FC

Founded: 1904
Former Names: Formed by the amalgamation of St. Sidwell United FC & Exeter United FC
Nickname: 'Grecians'
Ground: St. James Park, Exeter, EX4 6PX
Ground Capacity: 8,977
Seating Capacity: 3,806
Record Attendance: 20,984 (4/3/31)

Pitch Size: 113 × 71 yards
Colours: Red and White striped shirts, Black shorts
Telephone Nº: (01392) 411243
Ticket Office: (01392) 411243
Fax Number: (01392) 413959
Web Site: www.exetercityfc.co.uk

GENERAL INFORMATION
Car Parking: King William Street
Coach Parking: Paris Street Bus Station
Nearest Railway Station: Exeter St. James Park (adjacent)
Nearest Bus Station: Paris Street Bus Station
Club Shop: At the ground
Opening Times: Weekdays 10.00am to 5.00pm and Matchdays from 10.00am until kick-off
Telephone Nº: (01392) 411243
Police Telephone Nº: (0990) 700400

GROUND INFORMATION
Away Supporters' Entrances & Sections:
St. James Road turnstiles for standing in the St. James Road End or Well Street for seating in the Stagecoach Family Stand

ADMISSION INFO (2007/2008 PRICES)
Adult Standing: £13.00
Adult Seating: £15.00 – £16.00
Senior Citizen/Child Standing: £6.00 – £8.00
Senior Citizen/Child Seating: £6.00 – £10.00
Programme Price: £2.70

DISABLED INFORMATION
Wheelchairs: Accommodated in the Doble Stand and Cliff Bastin Stand
Helpers: One helper admitted per wheelchair
Prices: Free of charge for disabled. Normal prices for helpers
Disabled Toilets: Available by the Cliff Bastin Stand
Contact: (01392) 411243 (Bookings are necessary)

Travelling Supporters' Information:
Routes: From the North: Exit the M5 at Junction 30 and follow signs to the City Centre along Sidmouth Road and onto Heavitree Road. Take the 4th exit at the roundabout into Western Way and the 2nd exit into Tiverton Road then next left into St. James Road; From the East: Take the A30 into Heavitree Road (then as from the North); From the South & West: Take the A38 and follow City Centre signs into Western Way, then take the third exit at the roundabout into St. James Road.
Note: This ground is very difficult to find being in a residential area on the side of a hill without prominent floodlights.

FARSLEY CELTIC FC

Founded: 1908
Former Names: None
Nickname: 'Villagers'
Ground: Throstle Nest, Newlands, Farsley, Leeds, LS28 5BE
Record Attendance: 2,462 (2001)
Pitch Size: 110 × 67 yards

Colours: Blue shirts and shorts
Telephone Nº: (0113) 255-7292
Fax Number: (0113) 256-1517
Ground Capacity: 4,000
Seating Capacity: 500
Web site: www.farsleyceltic.co.uk
e-mail: farsleyceltic1908@supanet.com

GENERAL INFORMATION

Car Parking: Available at the ground
Coach Parking: Available at the ground
Nearest Railway Station: New Pudsey (1 mile)
Nearest Bus Station: Pudsey (1 mile)
Club Shop: At the ground
Opening Times: Weekday evenings 6.00pm – 11.00pm and weekends noon until 11.00pm
Telephone Nº: (0113) 255-7292

GROUND INFORMATION

Away Supporters' Entrances & Sections:
No usual segregation

ADMISSION INFO (2007/2008 PRICES)

Adult Standing: £10.00
Adult Seating: £12.00
Senior Citizen Standing: £5.00
Senior Citizen Seating: £6.00
Child Standing: £5.00
Child Seating: £6.00
Programme Price: £2.00

DISABLED INFORMATION

Wheelchairs: Accommodated
Helpers: Please phone the club for information
Prices: Please phone the club for information
Disabled Toilets: Available
Contact: (0113) 255-7292 (Bookings are necessary)

Travelling Supporters' Information:
Routes: From the North: Take the A1 to Wetherby then the A58 to Leeds. After about 8 miles take the 3rd exit at the roundabout onto the A6120 Ring Road. Follow signs for Bradford for approximately 12 miles and at the 7th roundabout take the B6157 signposted Stanningley. Continue for ½ mile passing the Police Station on the left then turn left down New Street (at the Tradex Warehouse). Turn right into Newlands and the ground is situated at the end of the road next to a new housing development.

FOREST GREEN ROVERS FC |

Founded: 1890
Former Names: Stroud FC
Nickname: 'The Rovers'
Ground: The New Lawn, Nympsfield Road, Forest Green, Nailsworth, Gloucestershire, GL6 0ET
Record Attendance: 3,021 (6th October 2006)
Pitch Size: 110 × 70 yards

Colours: Black and White striped shirts, Black shorts
Telephone Nº: (01453) 834860
Fax Number: (01453) 835291
Ground Capacity: 5,147
Seating Capacity: 2,500
Web site: www.fgrfc.co.uk

GENERAL INFORMATION

Supporters Club: Bob Savage, c/o Club
Telephone Nº: (01453) 834860
Car Parking: At the ground
Coach Parking: At the ground
Nearest Railway Station: Stroud
Nearest Bus Station: Nailsworth
Club Shop: At the ground
Opening Times: Matchdays only
Telephone Nº: (01453) 834860
Police Telephone Nº: 0845 090-1234

GROUND INFORMATION

Away Supporters' Entrances & Sections:
South Stand

ADMISSION INFO (2007/2008 PRICES)

Adult Standing: £12.00
Adult Seating: £14.00
Senior Citizen Standing: £8.00
Senior Citizen Seating: £10.00
Child Standing: £5.00
Child Seating: £7.00
Programme Price: £2.50

DISABLED INFORMATION

Wheelchairs: Accommodated in the Main Stand
Helpers: Admitted
Prices: Normal prices for the disabled. Free for helpers
Disabled Toilets: Yes
Contact: (01453) 834860 (Enquiries necessary at least 72 hours in advance)

Travelling Supporters' Information:
Routes: The ground is located 4 miles south of Stroud on the A46 to Bath. Upon entering Nailsworth, turn into Spring Hill at the mini-roundabout and the ground is approximately ½ mile up the hill on the left.

GRAYS ATHLETIC FC

Founded: 1890
Former Names: None
Nickname: 'The Blues'
Ground: The New Recreation Ground, Bridge Road, Grays, Essex RM17 6BZ
Record Attendance: 9,500 (1959)
Pitch Size: 110 × 71 yards

Colours: Sky Blue shirts and shorts
Telephone Nº: (01375) 377753
Fax Number: (01375) 391649
Ground Capacity: 4,000
Seating Capacity: 900
Web site: www.graysathletic.co.uk

GENERAL INFORMATION

Supporters Association: c/o Club
Telephone Nº: (01375) 377753
Car Parking: Town Centre Car Parks close to the ground
Coach Parking: Car Parks close to the ground
Nearest Railway Station: Grays
Nearest Bus Station: Grays
Club Shop: At the ground
Opening Times: Matchdays only
Telephone Nº: (01375) 377753
Police Telephone Nº: (01375) 391212

GROUND INFORMATION

Away Supporters' Entrances & Sections:
Bradbourne Road entrances and accommodation just off Clarence Road

ADMISSION INFO (2007/2008 PRICES)

Adult Standing: £13.00
Adult Seating: £13.00
Concessionary Standing: £8.00
Concessionary Seating: £8.00
Student Standing/Seating: £10.00
Junior Blues Club (Under-8s): £10.00 per season
Programme Price: £2.00

DISABLED INFORMATION

Wheelchairs: Accommodated in the Main Stand
Helpers: One admitted free of charge per disabled fan
Prices: Please phone the club for information
Disabled Toilets: Three available
Contact: (01375) 391649

Travelling Supporters' Information:
Routes: Exit the M25 at Junction 30 and take the A13 towards Southend. At the Grays exit, follow signs to the town centre. Upon reaching the one-way system, keep to the left and continue uphill for about ½ miles before turning right into Bridge Road. The ground is then on the right.

HALIFAX TOWN FC

Founded: 1911
Nickname: 'Shaymen'
Ground: Shay Stadium, Shay Syke, Halifax HX1 2YS
Ground Capacity: 6,561
Seating Capacity: 2,912
Record Attendance: 36,885 (14/2/53)
Pitch Size: 110 × 74 yards

Colours: Blue and White shirts with White shorts
Telephone No: (01422) 341222
Ticket Office: (01422) 341222
Fax Number: (01422) 349487
Web Site: www.halifaxafc.co.uk
E-mail: theshay@halifaxafc.co.uk

GENERAL INFORMATION

Car Parking: Shaw Hill Car Park (Nearby)
Coach Parking: Shaw Hill
Nearest Railway Station: Halifax (10 minutes walk)
Nearest Bus Station: Halifax (20 minutes walk)
Club Shop: At the ground
Opening Times: Please phone for details
Telephone No: (01422) 341222

GROUND INFORMATION

Away Supporters' Entrances & Sections:
North Stand

ADMISSION INFO (2007/2008 PRICES)

Adult Standing: £15.00
Adult Seating: £15.00
Under-16s/Senior Citizen Standing/Seating: £8.00
Ages 8 to 11 Standing/Seating: £5.00
Ages 7 and Under: Free of charge
Programme Price: £2.50

DISABLED INFORMATION

Wheelchairs: 10 spaces available in the disabled section,
12 spaces available on the new North Terrace
Facilities for the visually impaired may be available.
Helpers: One admitted free with each paying disabled fan
Prices: Normal prices apply for the disabled.
Disabled Toilets: In the Main Stand and the new North and
South Terraces
Contact: (01422) 434212 (Bookings are not necessary)

Travelling Supporters' Information:
Routes: From the North: Take the A629 to Halifax Town Centre. Take the 2nd exit at the roundabout into Broad Street and follow signs for Huddersfield (A629) into Skircoat Road; From the South, East and West: Exit the M62 at Junction 24 and follow Halifax (A629) signs for the Town Centre into Skircoat Road then Shaw Hill for ground.

HISTON FC

Founded: 1904
Former Names: Histon Institute FC
Nickname: 'The Stutes'
Ground: The Glass World Stadium, Bridge Road, Impington, Cambridge CB4 9PH
Record Attendance: 6,400 (1956)
Pitch Size: 110 × 75 yards

Colours: Red shirts with Black shorts
Telephone Nº: (01223) 237373
Fax Number: (01223) 237373
Ground Capacity: 3,750
Seating Capacity: 700
Web site: www.histonfc.co.uk

GENERAL INFORMATION
Supporters Club: Yes
Telephone Nº: (01223) 846455 (Jenny Wells)
Car Parking: Permit holders and disabled parking only at the ground
Coach Parking: For team coaches only
Nearest Railway Station: Cambridge (3 miles)
Nearest Bus Station: Cambridge (3 miles) (Service 107)
Club Shop: At the ground
Opening Times: Saturday matchdays 12.30pm – 6.00pm, Evening matches 6.00pm – 11.00pm
Telephone Nº: (01223) 237373

GROUND INFORMATION
Away Supporters' Entrances & Sections:
No usual segregation

ADMISSION INFO (2007/2008 PRICES)
Adult Standing: £12.00
Adult Seating: £13.00
Child Standing: £3.00
Child Seating: £3.00
Senior Citizen Standing: £7.00
Senior Citizen Seating: £8.00
Programme Price: £2.00

DISABLED INFORMATION
Wheelchairs: Accommodated
Helpers: Please contact the club for details
Prices: The disabled are charged concessionary prices
Disabled Toilets: Available
Contact: (01223) 237373 (Bookings are not necessary)

Travelling Supporters' Information:
Routes: Exit the M11 at Junction 14 and follow the A14 eastwards. Take the first exit onto the B1049 (signposted Histon & Cottenham). Turn left at the traffic lights at the top of the slip road and pass the Holiday Inn on the right. Continue over the bridge and the entrance to the ground is on the right.

KIDDERMINSTER HARRIERS FC

Founded: 1886
Nickname: 'Harriers'
Ground: Aggborough, Hoo Road, Kidderminster, Worcestershire DY10 1NB
Ground Capacity: 6,444
Seating Capacity: 3,143
Record Attendance: 9,155 (1948)

Pitch Size: 110 × 72 yards
Colours: Red shirts with White shorts
Telephone Nº: (01562) 823931
Fax Number: (01562) 827329
Web Site: www.harriers.co.uk

GENERAL INFORMATION

Car Parking: At the ground
Coach Parking: As directed
Nearest Railway Station: Kidderminster
Nearest Bus Station: Kidderminster Town Centre
Club Shop: At the ground
Opening Times: Weekdays and First Team Matchdays 9.00am to 5.00pm
Telephone Nº: (01562) 823931
Police Telephone Nº: –

GROUND INFORMATION

Away Supporters' Entrances & Sections:
John Smiths Stand Entrance D and South Terrace Entrance E

ADMISSION INFO (2007/2008 PRICES)

Adult Standing: £13.00
Adult Seating: £16.00
Senior Citizen Standing: £8.00   **Under-16s**: £5.00
Concessionary Seating: £11.00
Note: Under-8s are admitted free with a paying adult
Programme Price: £2.50

DISABLED INFORMATION

Wheelchairs: Home fans accommodated at the front of the Main Stand, Away fans in front of the John Smiths Stand
Helpers: Admitted
Prices: £10.00 for each disabled fan plus one helper
Disabled Toilets: Available by the disabled area
Contact: (01562) 823931   (Bookings are not necessary)

Travelling Supporters' Information:
Routes: Exit the M5 at Junction 3 and follow the A456 to Kidderminster. The ground is situated close by the Severn Valley Railway Station so follow the brown Steam Train signs and turn into Hoo Road about 200 yards downhill of the station. Follow the road along for ¼ mile and the ground is on the left.

NORTHWICH VICTORIA FC

Founded: 1874
Former Names: None
Nickname: 'The Vics' 'The Greens' 'The Trickies'
Ground: Victoria Stadium, Wincham Avenue,
Wincham, Northwich   CW9 6GB
Record Attendance: –
Pitch Size: 112 × 74 yards

Colours: Green & White hooped shirts, White shorts
Office Telephone Nº: (01606) 41555
Fax Number: (01606) 41565
Ground Capacity: 5,046
Seating Capacity: 1,180
Web site: www.northwichvics.co.uk

GENERAL INFORMATION
Supporters Club: Dave Thomas, c/o Club
Telephone Nº: (01606) 41555
Car Parking: Ample parking spaces available at the ground
Coach Parking: At the ground
Nearest Railway Station: Northwich (2½ miles)
Nearest Bus Station: Northwich (2½ miles)
Club Shop: At the ground
Opening Times: Weekdays & Matchdays 10.00am–4.00pm
Telephone Nº: (01606) 41555
Police Telephone Nº: (01606) 48000

GROUND INFORMATION
Away Supporters' Entrances & Sections: West Terrace

ADMISSION INFO (2006/2007 PRICES)
Adult Standing: £12.00
Adult Seating: £14.00
Senior Citizen Standing: £10.00
Senior Citizen Seating: £12.00
Under-16s Standing: £5.00
Under-16s Seating: £7.00
Under-12s Standing/Seating: £2.50
Programme Price: £2.00

DISABLED INFORMATION
Wheelchairs: 52 spaces are available in total
Helpers: Admitted
Prices: Free for the disabled. Helpers pay normal prices
Disabled Toilets: Yes
Contact: (01606) 41555   (Please phone to book)

Travelling Supporters' Information:
Routes: Exit the M6 at Junction 19 and take the A556 towards Northwich. After 3 miles turn right onto the A559 following signs for Warrington. Turn left after Marston opposite the Black Greyhound Inn then left into Wincham Avenue after 200 yards.
Alternative Route: Exit the M56 at Junction 10 and take the A559 to the Black Greyhound Inn then turn right. Then as above

OXFORD UNITED FC

Founded: 1893 (**Entered League**: 1962)
Former Names: Headington United FC (1893-1960)
Nickname: 'U's'
Ground: Kassam Stadium, Grenoble Road, Oxford, OX4 4XP
Ground Capacity: 12,500 (All seats)
Record Attendance: 22,730 (At the Manor Ground)

Pitch Size: 115 × 71 yards
Colours: Yellow shirts with Navy Blue shorts
Telephone Nº: (01865) 337500
Ticket Office: (01865) 337533
Fax Number: (01865) 337555
Web Site: www.oufc.co.uk

GENERAL INFORMATION

Car Parking: 2,000 free spaces available at the ground
Coach Parking: At the ground
Nearest Railway Station: Oxford (4 miles)
Nearest Bus Station: Oxford
Club Shop: At the ground
Opening Times: Monday to Friday 10.00 – 5.00pm; Saturdays 10am – 4.00pm (Matchdays until 2.45pm)
Telephone Nº: (01865) 335310
Police Telephone Nº: (01865) 749909

GROUND INFORMATION

Away Supporters' Entrances & Sections:
North Stand turnstiles for North Stand accommodation. Ticket office for away supporters is adjacent

ADMISSION INFO (2007/2008 PRICES)

Adult Seating: £16.00 – £19.50
Under-16s Seating: £5.50 – £13.00
Senior Citizen Seating: £8.50 – £13.00
Note: Discounts are available for advance bookings
Programme Price: £2.50

DISABLED INFORMATION

Wheelchairs: Accommodated in areas in the North, East and South Stands
Helpers: One helper admitted per disabled person
Prices: Normal prices for the disabled. One helper admitted free of charge per disabled fan if required
Disabled Toilets: Available
Commentaries are available for the visually impaired
Contact: (01865) 337533 (Bookings are not necessary)

Travelling Supporters' Information:
Routes: From the Oxford Ring Road take the A423 towards Henley and Reading then turn left after ½ mile following signs for the Oxford Science Park. Bear left and go straight on at two roundabouts then the Stadium is on the left in Grenoble Road. The Kassam Stadium is clearly signposted on all major roads in Oxford.

RUSHDEN & DIAMONDS FC

Founded: 1992   (**Entered League**: 2001)
Former Names: Formed by the amalgamation of Rushden Town FC and Irthlingborough Diamonds FC
Nickname: 'Diamonds'
Ground: Nene Park, Diamond Way, Irthlingborough, Northants   NN9 5QF
Ground Capacity: 6,441
Seating Capacity: 4,641

Record Attendance: 6,431   (vs Leeds United in 1999)
Pitch Size: 111 × 74 yards
Colours: White shirts, shorts and socks
Telephone Nº: (01933) 652000
Ticket Office Nº: (01933) 652936
Fax Number: (01933) 652606
Web Site: www.thediamondsfc.com

GENERAL INFORMATION

Car Parking: At the ground   (£3.00 charge)
Coach Parking: At the ground   (£10.00 charge)
Nearest Railway Station: Wellingborough (5 miles)
Nearest Bus Station: Wellingborough
Club Shop: Yes – at the 'Doc' Shop
Opening Times: Weekdays 10.00am to 5.00pm; Saturday matchdays 10.00am to 2.50pm and 4.45pm to 5.30pm; Midweek matchdays 10.00am to 7.40pm
Telephone Nº: (01933) 652000
Police Telephone Nº: (01933) 440333

GROUND INFORMATION

Away Supporters' Entrances & Sections:
Airwair Stand

ADMISSION INFO (2007/2008 PRICES)

Adult Standing: £13.00 (Home fans only)
Adult Seating: £16.00
Concessionary Standing: £8.00
Concessionary Seating: £11.00
Under-16s Standing/Seating: £5.00
Note: Under-8s are admitted free with a paying adult
Programme Price: £2.50

DISABLED INFORMATION

Wheelchairs: Accommodated around the ground
Helpers: Admitted
Prices: £8.00 – £11.00 for the disabled with registered carers admitted free of charge
Disabled Toilets: Available around the ground
Contact: (01933) 652936 Matt Banyard (Bookings are preferred)

Travelling Supporters' Information:
Routes: The ground is located on the A6 about 350 yards north of the junction with the A45 (over the bridge). This is approximately 6 miles south of the A14.

22

SALISBURY CITY FC

Founded: 1947
Former Names: Salisbury FC
Nickname: 'The Whites'
Ground: The Raymond McEnhill Stadium, Partridge Way, Old Sarum, Salisbury, Wiltshire SP4 6PU
Record Attendance: 3,100 (3rd December 2006)
Pitch Size: 115 × 76 yards

Colours: White shirts with Black shorts
Telephone Nº: (01722) 326454
Fax Number: (01722) 323100
Ground Capacity: 3,740
Seating Capacity: 450
Web site:
www.salisburyjournal.co.uk/sport/salisburycityfc

GENERAL INFORMATION

Car Parking: At the ground
Coach Parking: At the ground
Nearest Railway Station: Salisbury (4 miles)
Nearest Bus Station: Salisbury
Club Shop: At the ground + an online shop
Opening Times: Office Hours and Matchdays
Telephone Nº: (01722) 326454
Postal Sales: Yes
Police Telephone Nº: (01722) 411444

GROUND INFORMATION

Away Supporters' Entrances & Sections:
Portway End entrances and accommodation

ADMISSION INFO (2007/2008 PRICES)

Adult Standing: £10.00
Adult Seating: £12.00
Senior Citizen Standing: £7.00
Senior Citizen Seating: £9.00
Child Standing: Free of charge with a paying adult
Child Seating: £2.00
Programme Price: £2.00

DISABLED INFORMATION

Wheelchairs: Accommodated in a special area in the Main Stand. A stairlift is available.
Helpers: Admitted
Prices: Normal prices apply
Disabled Toilets: Available
Contact: (01722) 326454 (Bookings are necessary)

Travelling Supporters' Information:
Routes: The Stadium well signposted and is situated off the main A345 Salisbury to Amesbury road on the northern edge of the City, 2 miles from the City Centre.

STAFFORD RANGERS FC

Founded: 1876
Former Names: None
Nickname: 'The Boro'
Ground: Marston Road, Stafford   ST16 3BX
Record Attendance: 8,523 (4/1/75)
Pitch Size: 112 × 75 yards

Colours: Black and White striped shirts, Black shorts
Telephone Nº: (01785) 602430
Social Club Nº: (01785) 602432
Ground Capacity: 4,250
Seating Capacity: 2,157
Web site: www.staffordrangers.co.uk

GENERAL INFORMATION
Supporters Club: c/o Social Club
Telephone Nº: (01785) 602432
Car Parking: At the ground
Coach Parking: Astonfields Road
Nearest Railway Station: Stafford (1½ miles)
Nearest Bus Station: Stafford
Club Shop: At the ground
Opening Times: Matchdays only
Telephone Nº: (01785) 602430
Police Telephone Nº: (01785) 258151

GROUND INFORMATION
Away Supporters' Entrances & Sections:
Lotus End

ADMISSION INFO (2007/2008 PRICES)
Adult Standing: £12.00
Adult Seating: £14.00
Concessionary Standing: £8.00
Concessionary Seating: £10.00
Children under the age of 12 are admitted for £2.00 when accompanied by a paying adult
Programme Price: £2.50

DISABLED INFORMATION
Wheelchairs: Accommodated at Marston Road End
Helpers: Admitted
Prices: Concessionary prices for the disabled. Normal prices for helpers
Disabled Toilets: Available
Contact: (01785) 602430   (Bookings are not necessary)

Travelling Supporters' Information:
Routes: Exit the M6 at Junction 14 and take the slip road signposted 'Stone/Stafford'. Continue to traffic island and go straight across then take the 3rd exit on the right into Common Road, signposted 'Common Road/Aston Fields Industrial Estate'. Follow the road to the bridge and bear left over the bridge. The ground is on the right.

STEVENAGE BOROUGH FC

Founded: 1976
Former Names: None
Nickname: 'Boro'
Ground: Stevenage Stadium, Broadhall Way, Stevenage, Hertfordshire   SG2 8RH
Record Attendance: 8,040 (25/1/98)
Pitch Size: 110 × 70 yards

Colours: Red and White shirts with Red shorts
Telephone N°: (01438) 223223
Daytime Phone N°: (01438) 223223
Fax Number: (01438) 743666
Ground Capacity: 7,104
Seating Capacity: 3,404
Web site: www.stevenageborofc.com

GENERAL INFORMATION

Supporters Club: Mervyn Stoke Geddis, 21 Woodland Way, Stevenage
Telephone N°: (01438) 313236
Car Parking: Fairlands Show Ground (opposite)
Coach Parking: At the ground
Nearest Railway Station: Stevenage (1 mile)
Nearest Bus Station: Stevenage
Club Shop: At the ground
Opening Times: Tuesday to Thursday and matchdays 10.00am to 5.00pm
Telephone N°: 0870 811-2494
Police Telephone N°: (01438) 757000

GROUND INFORMATION

Away Supporters' Entrances & Sections:
South Terrace entrances and accommodation

ADMISSION INFO (2007/2008 PRICES)

Adult Standing: £12.00
Adult Seating: £15.00
Child Standing: £5.00
Senior Citizen Standing: £10.00
Senior Citizen/Child Seating: £12.00
Programme Price: £2.50

DISABLED INFORMATION

Wheelchairs: 10 spaces available in total by the North Terrace
Helpers: Admitted
Prices: £9.00 for the disabled. Free of charge for helpers
Disabled Toilets: Yes
Contact: (01438) 223223   (Bookings are necessary)

Travelling Supporters' Information:
Routes: Exit the A1(M) at Junction 7 and take the B197. The ground is on the right at the 2nd roundabout.
Bus Routes: SB4 and SB5

TORQUAY UNITED FC

Founded: 1899
Former Name: Torquay Town FC (1899-1910)
Nickname: 'Gulls'
Ground: Plainmoor Ground, Torquay TQ1 3PS
Ground Capacity: 6,117
Seating Capacity: 2,240
Record Attendance: 21,908 (29/1/55)

Pitch Size: 110 × 74 yards
Colours: Shirts are Yellow with Royal Blue trim, shorts and socks are Yellow
Telephone Nº: (01803) 328666
Ticket Office: (01803) 328666
Fax Number: (01803) 323976
Web Site: www.torquayunited.com

GENERAL INFORMATION
Car Parking: Street parking
Coach Parking: Lymington Road Coach Station (½ mile)
Nearest Railway Station: Torquay (2 miles)
Nearest Bus Station: Lymington Road (½ mile)
Club Shop: At the ground
Opening Times: Matchdays and during Office Hours
Telephone Nº: (01803) 328666
Police Telephone Nº: 0845 277-7444

GROUND INFORMATION
Away Supporters' Entrances & Sections:
Babbacombe End turnstiles for Babbacombe End

ADMISSION INFO (2007/2008 PRICES)
Adult Standing: £14.00
Adult Seating: £15.00
Concessionary Standing: £11.00 (Under-16s £5.00)
Concessionary Seating: £12.00 (Under-16s £5.00)
Programme Price: £2.00

DISABLED INFORMATION
Wheelchairs: 15 spaces in front of Ellacombe End Stand
Helpers: One helper admitted per wheelchair
Prices: Normal prices for the disabled. Free for helpers
Disabled Toilets: 2 available within the Main Stand
Audio facilities are available for the blind
Contact: (01803) 328666 (Bookings necessary for the blind)

Travelling Supporters' Information:
Routes: From the North and East: Take the M5 to the A38 then A380 to Torquay. On entering Torquay, turn left at the 1st set of traffic lights after Riviera Way Retail Park into Hele Road. Following signs for the ground, continue straight on over two mini-roundabouts, go up West Hill Road to the traffic lights, then straight ahead into Warbro Road. The ground is situated on the right after 200 yards.

WEYMOUTH FC

Founded: 1890
Former Names: None
Nickname: 'Terras'
Ground: Wessex Stadium, Radipole Lane, Weymouth, Dorset DT4 9XJ
Record Attendance: 6,500 (14th November 2005)
Pitch Size: 115 × 74 yards

Colours: Shirts are Claret and Sky Blue, Claret shorts
Telephone Nº: (01305) 785558
Fax Number: (01305) 766658
Ground Capacity: 6,500
Seating Capacity: 800
Web site: www.theterras.co.uk

GENERAL INFORMATION

Supporters Club: Nigel Beckett, c/o Club
Telephone Nº: (01305) 785558
Car Parking: 200 spaces available at the ground
Coach Parking: At the ground
Nearest Railway Station: Weymouth (2 miles)
Nearest Bus Station: Weymouth Town Centre
Club Shop: At the ground
Opening Times: Matchdays only
Telephone Nº: –
Police Telephone Nº: (01305) 251212

GROUND INFORMATION

Away Supporters' Entrances & Sections:
Visitors End turnstiles and accommodation when segregation is used

ADMISSION INFO (2007/2008 PRICES)

Adult Standing: £13.00
Adult Seating: £15.00
Senior Citizen/Student Standing: £8.00
Senior Citizen/Student Seating: £10.00
Under-16s Standing: £5.00
Under-16s Seating: £7.00
Programme Price: £2.00

DISABLED INFORMATION

Wheelchairs: Accommodated
Helpers: Admitted
Prices: Normal prices apply for the disabled. Free for helpers
Disabled Toilets: Yes
Contact: (01305) 785558 (Bookings are not necessary)

Travelling Supporters' Information:
Routes: Take the A354 from Dorchester to Weymouth and turn right at the first roundabout to the town centre. Take the 3rd exit at the next roundabout and follow signs for the ground which is about ½ mile on the right.

WOKING FC

Founded: 1889	**Colours**: Shirts are Red & White halves, Black shorts
Former Names: None	**Telephone Nº**: (01483) 772470
Nickname: 'Cardinals'	**Daytime Phone Nº**: (01483) 772470
Ground: Kingfield Stadium, Kingfield, Woking, Surrey GU22 9AA	**Fax Number**: (01483) 888423
	Ground Capacity: 6,161
Record Attendance: 6,000 (1997)	**Seating Capacity**: 2,511
Pitch Size: 109 × 76 yards	**Web site**: www.wokingfc.co.uk

GENERAL INFORMATION

Supporters Club: Mr. G. Burnett (Secretary), c/o Club
Telephone Nº: (01483) 772470
Car Parking: Limited parking at the ground
Coach Parking: At or opposite the ground
Nearest Railway Station: Woking (1 mile)
Nearest Bus Station: Woking
Club Shop: At the ground
Opening Times: Weekdays and Matchdays
Telephone Nº: (01483) 772470
Police Telephone Nº: (01483) 761991

GROUND INFORMATION

Away Supporters' Entrances & Sections:
Kingfield Road when segregation is in force

ADMISSION INFO (2007/2008 PRICES)

Adult Standing: £12.00
Adult Seating: £15.00
Child Standing: £5.00
Child Seating: £6.00
Senior Citizen Standing: £10.00
Senior Citizen Seating: £11.00
Programme Price: £2.50

DISABLED INFORMATION

Wheelchairs: 8 spaces in the Leslie Gosden Stand and 8 spaces in front of the Family Stand
Helpers: Admitted
Prices: One wheelchair and helper for £11.00
Disabled Toilets: Yes – in the Leslie Gosden Stand and Family Stand area
Contact: (01483) 772470 (Bookings are necessary)

Travelling Supporters' Information:
Routes: Exit the M25 at Junction 10 and follow the A3 towards Guildford. Leave at the next junction onto the B2215 through Ripley and join the A247 to Woking. Alternatively, exit the M25 at Junction 11 and follow the A320 to Woking Town Centre. The ground is on the outskirts of Woking – follow signs on the A320 and A247.

YORK CITY FC

Founded: 1922
Nickname: 'Minstermen'
Ground: Kit Kat Crescent, York   YO30 7AQ
Ground Capacity: 9,496
Seating Capacity: 3,509
Record Attendance: 28,123 (5/3/38)
Pitch Size: 115 × 74 yards

Colours: Red shirts with White shorts
Telephone Nº: (0870) 7771922
Ticket Office: (0870) 7771922 Extension 1
Fax Number: (0870) 7741993
Web Site: www.ycfc.net

GENERAL INFORMATION

Car Parking: Street parking
Coach Parking: By Police direction
Nearest Railway Station: York (1 mile)
Nearest Bus Station: York
Club Shop: At the ground
Opening Times: Weekdays 10.30am – 2.30pm and
Saturday Matchdays 1.00pm–3.00pm and 4.40pm–5.30pm
Telephone Nº: (0870) 7771922 Extension 4
Police Telephone Nº: 0845 606-0247

GROUND INFORMATION

Away Supporters' Entrances & Sections:
Grosvenor Road turnstiles for Grosvenor Road End

ADMISSION INFO (2007/2008 PRICES)

Adult Standing: £14.00
Adult Seating: £15.00 – £17.00
Child Standing: £9.00
Child Seating: £6.00 – £11.00
Note: Concessions are available in the Family Stand
Programme Price: £2.50

DISABLED INFORMATION

Wheelchairs: 18 spaces in total for Home and Away fans in
the disabled section, in front of the Social Club
Helpers: One helper admitted per disabled person
Prices: £14.00 for the disabled. Free of charge for helpers
Disabled Toilets: Available at entrance to the disabled area
Contact: (0870) 7771922 (Ext. 1) (Bookings not necessary)

Travelling Supporters' Information:
Routes: From the North: Take the A1 then the A59 following signs for York. Cross the railway bridge and turn left after 2 miles into Water End. Turn right at the end following City Centre signs for nearly ½ mile then turn left into Bootham Crescent; From the South: Take the A64 and turn left after Buckles Inn onto the Outer Ring Road. Turn right onto the A19, follow City Centre signs for 1½ miles then turn left into Bootham Crescent; From the East: Take the Outer Ring Road turning left onto the A19. Then as from the South; From the West: Take the Outer Ring Road turning right onto the A19. Then as from the South.

THE FOOTBALL CONFERENCE BLUE SQUARE NORTH

Address

Riverside House, 14B High Street,
Crayford, Kent   DA1   4HG

Phone (01322) 411021   **Fax** (01322) 411022

Web site   www.footballconference.co.uk

Clubs for the 2007/2008 Season

AFC TELFORD UNITED

Founded: 2004
Former Names: Formed after Telford United FC went out of business
Nickname: 'The Bucks'
Ground: The New Bucks Head Stadium, Watling Street, Wellington, Telford   TF1 2TU
Record Attendance: 13,000 (1935)

Pitch Size: 110 × 74 yards
Colours: White shirts with Black shorts
Telehone Nº: (01952) 640064
Fax Number: (01952) 640021
Ground Capacity: 6,800
Seating Capacity: 2,128
Web site: www.telfordutd.co.uk

GENERAL INFORMATION

Supporters Club: None
Car Parking: At the ground
Coach Parking: At the ground
Nearest Railway Station: Wellington and Telford Central
Nearest Bus Station: –
Club Shop: At the ground
Opening Times: Matchdays only 10.00am – 4.00pm
Telephone Nº: –
Police Telephone Nº: 08457 444888

GROUND INFORMATION

Away Supporters' Entrances & Sections:
South Stand on the rare occasion when segregation is used

ADMISSION INFO (2007/2008 PRICES)

Adult Standing: £9.00
Adult Seating: £10.00
Child Standing: £1.00
Child Seating: £1.00
Senior Citizen/Concessionary Standing: £6.00
Senior Citizen/Concessionary Seating: £7.00
Programme Price: £2.00

DISABLED INFORMATION

Wheelchairs: Accommodated at the both ends of the ground
Helpers: Admitted
Prices: Normal prices apply
Disabled Toilets: Available
Contact: (01952) 640064   (Bookings are not necessary)

Travelling Supporters' Information:
Routes: Exit the M54 at Junction 6 and take the A518. Go straight on at the first roundabout, take the second exit at the next roundabout then turn left at the following roundabout. Turn right immediately after the railway bridge for the ground.

ALFRETON TOWN FC

Founded: 1959
Former Names: None
Nickname: 'Reds'
Ground: The Impact Arena, North Street, Alfreton, Derbyshire
Record Attendance: 5,023 vs Matlock Town (1960)
Pitch Size: 110 × 75 yards

Colours: Red shirts and shorts
Telephone Nº: (01773) 830277
Fax Number: (01773) 836164
Ground Capacity: 5,000
Seating Capacity: 1,600
Web site: www.alfretontownfc.com

GENERAL INFORMATION

Supporters Club: Mark Thorpe, c/o Social Club
Telephone Nº: (01773) 836251
Car Parking: At the ground
Coach Parking: At the ground
Nearest Railway Station: Alfreton (½ mile)
Nearest Bus Station: Alfreton (5 minutes walk)
Club Shop: At the ground
Opening Times: Matchdays (including Youth & Reserves)
Telephone Nº: (01773) 830277
Police Telephone Nº: (01773) 570100

GROUND INFORMATION

Away Supporters' Entrances & Sections:
No usual segregation

ADMISSION INFO (2007/2008 PRICES)

Adult Standing: £9.00
Adult Seating: £9.00
Senior Citizen/Junior Standing: £4.50
Senior Citizen/Junior Seating: £4.50
Programme Price: £2.00

DISABLED INFORMATION

Wheelchairs: Accommodated at the front of the Stand
Helpers: Admitted
Prices: Please phone the club for information
Disabled Toilets: Available in the Executive Bar
Contact: (01773) 830277 (Bookings are not necessary)

Travelling Supporters' Information:
Routes: Exit the M1 at Junction 28 and take the A38 signposted for Derby. After 2 miles take the sliproad onto the B600 then go right at the main road towards the town centre. After ½ mile turn left down North Street and the ground is on the right after 200 yards.

BARROW FC

Founded: 1901
Former Names: None
Nickname: 'Bluebirds'
Ground: Holker Street Stadium, Barrow-in-Furness, Cumbria   LA14 5UQ
Record Attendance: 16,874 (1954)
Pitch Size: 110 × 75 yards

Colours: Blue and White shirts with Blue shorts
Matchday Telephone Nº: (01229) 820346
Weekday Telephone Nº: (01229) 823061
Fax Number: (01229) 820346/823061
Ground Capacity: 5,000
Seating Capacity: 1,064
Web site: www.barrowafc.com

GENERAL INFORMATION

Supporters Club: Bill Ablitt, c/o Club
Telephone Nº: (01229) 471617
Car Parking: Street Parking, Popular Side Car Park and Soccer Bar Car Park
Coach Parking: Adjacent to the ground
Nearest Railway Station: Barrow Central (½ mile)
Nearest Bus Station: ½ mile
Club Shop: 60 Buccleuch Street, Barrow-in-Furness, LA14 1QG
Opening Times: Monday to Wednesday & Fridays 10.00am – 4.00pm, Saturdays 10.00am – 2.00pm
Telephone Nº: (01229) 823061 (weekdays)
Police Telephone Nº: (01229) 824532

GROUND INFORMATION

Away Supporters' Entrances & Sections:
West Terrace (not covered)

ADMISSION INFO (2007/2008 PRICES)

Adult Standing: £9.00
Adult Seating: £10.00
Concessionary Standing: £6.00
Concessionary Seating: £7.00
Under-14s: £3.00
Programme Price: £1.50

DISABLED INFORMATION

Wheelchairs: 6 spaces available in the Disabled Area
Helpers: Admitted
Prices: Normal prices apply
Disabled Toilets: Available
Contact: (01229) 820346   (Bookings are not necessary)

Travelling Supporters' Information:
Routes: Exit the M6 at Junction 36 and take the A590 through Ulverston. Using the bypass, follow signs for Barrow. After approximately 5 miles, turn left into Wilkie Road and the ground is on the left.

BLYTH SPARTANS FC

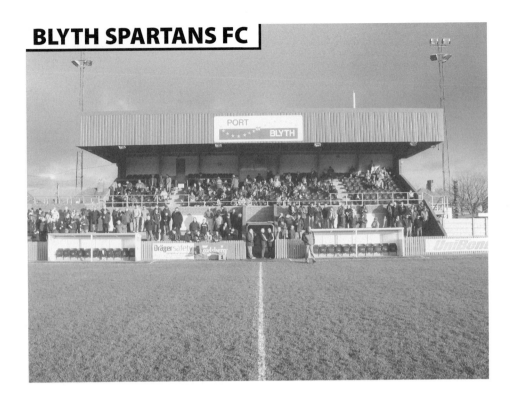

Founded: 1899
Former Names: None
Nickname: 'Spartans'
Ground: Croft Park, Blyth, Northumberland, NE24 3JE
Record Attendance: 10,186
Pitch Size: 110 × 70 yards

Colours: Green and White striped shirts, Black shorts
Telephone Nº: (01670) 352373 (Office)
Fax Number: (01670) 545592
Ground Capacity: 6,000
Seating Capacity: 540
Web site: www.blythspartansafc.co.uk

GENERAL INFORMATION

Supporters Club: Bobby Bell, c/o Club
Telephone Nº: (01670) 352373
Car Parking: At the ground
Coach Parking: At the ground
Nearest Railway Station: Newcastle
Nearest Bus Station: Blyth (5 minutes walk)
Club Shop: At the ground
Opening Times: Matchdays only
Telephone Nº: c/o (01670) 336379
Police Telephone Nº: (01661) 872555

GROUND INFORMATION

Away Supporters' Entrances & Sections:
No usual segregation

ADMISSION INFO (2007/2008 PRICES)

Adult Standing: £9.00
Adult Seating: £10.00
Child Standing: £5.00
Child Seating: £6.00
Programme Price: £1.50

DISABLED INFORMATION

Wheelchairs: Accommodated
Helpers: Please phone the club for information
Prices: Please phone the club for information
Disabled Toilets: Yes
Contact: (01670) 352373 (Bookings are necessary)

Travelling Supporters' Information:
Routes: Pass through the Tyne Tunnel and take the left lane for Morpeth (A19/A1). At the 2nd roundabout (after approximately 7 miles) take full right turn for the A189 (signposted Ashington). After 2 miles take the slip road (A1061 signposted Blyth). Follow signs for Blyth turning left at the caravan site. At the 2nd roundabout turn right and the ground is on the left.

BOSTON UNITED FC

Founded: 1934
Former Names: Boston Town FC & Boston Swifts FC
Nickname: 'The Pilgrims'
Ground: The Staffsmart Stadium, York Street, Boston PE21 6HJ
Ground Capacity: 6,613 Seating Capacity: 2,000
Pitch Size: 112 × 72 yards

Record Attendance: 10,086 (1955)
Colours: Amber and Black shirts, Black shorts
Telephone Nº: (01205) 364406 (Office)
Matchday Info: (01205) 365525 (Answerphone)
Fax Number: (01205) 354063
Web Site: www.bufc.co.uk
E-mail: admin@bufc.co.uk

GENERAL INFORMATION

Car Parking: Permit holders only
Coach Parking: Available near to the ground
Nearest Railway Station: Boston (½ mile)
Nearest Bus Station: Boston Coach Station (¼ mile)
Club Shop: In the car park at the ground
Opening Times: Weekdays from 9.00am to 5.00pm, Saturdays from 2.00pm to 5.00pm
Telephone Nº: (01205) 364406
Police Telephone Nº: (01205) 366222

GROUND INFORMATION

Away Supporters' Entrances & Sections:
Town End Entrance gates 7 to 10

ADMISSION INFO (2007/2008 PRICES)

Adult Standing: £12.00
Adult Seating: £14.00
Child Standing: £6.00
Child Seating: £7.00
Senior Citizen Standing: £9.00
Senior Citizen Seating: £10.00
Programme Price: £2.50

DISABLED INFORMATION

Wheelchairs: 7 spaces available for home fans, 4 spaces for away fans below the Main Stand at the Town End
Helpers: One helper admitted per disabled fan
Prices: £10.00 for the disabled. Free of charge for helpers
Disabled Toilets: Available in the Town End Terrace
Contact: (01205) 364406 (Bookings are necessary)

Travelling Supporters' Information:
From the North: Take the A17 from Sleaford, bear right after the railway crossing to the traffic lights over the bridge. Go forward through the traffic lights into York Street for the ground; From the South: Take the A16 from Spalding and turn right at the traffic lights over the bridge. Go forward through the next traffic lights into York Street for the ground.

BURSCOUGH FC

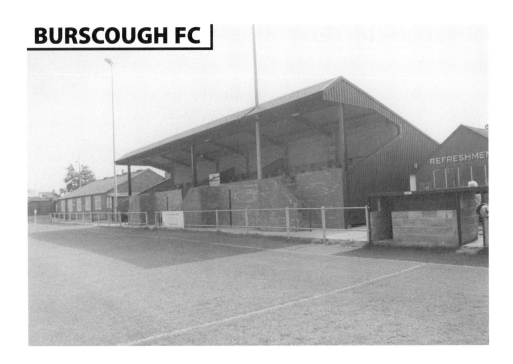

Founded: 1946
Former Names: None
Nickname: 'Linnets'
Ground: Victoria Park, Bobby Langton Way, Mart Lane, Burscough, Ormskirk, Lancs. L40 0SD
Record Attendance: 4,798 (vs Wigan Athletic)
Pitch Size: 110 × 70 yards

Colours: White and Green shirts, shorts and socks
Contact Nº: (01704) 880587
Fax Number: (01704) 893237
Ground Capacity: 2,500
Seating Capacity: 260
Web site: www.burscoughfc.co.uk
Club Information Nº: (01704) 893237

GENERAL INFORMATION
Supporters Club: Yes – contact the Club for details
Car Parking: Adjacent to the ground
Coach Parking: Adjacent to the ground
Nearest Railway Station: Burscough Bridge (200yds) or Burscough Junction (600 yards)
Nearest Bus Station: Ormskirk
Club Shop: At the ground
Opening Times: Matchdays only
Telephone Nº: –
Police Telephone Nº: (01704) 892181

GROUND INFORMATION
Away Supporters' Entrances & Sections:
Segregation only used when required

ADMISSION INFO (2007/2008 PRICES)
Adult Standing: £9.00
Adult Seating: £9.00
Child/Senior Citizen Standing: £5.00
Child/Senior Citizen Seating: £5.00
Programme Price: £1.50

DISABLED INFORMATION
Wheelchairs: Accommodated
Helpers: Admitted
Prices: Normal prices apply for disabled and helpers
Disabled Toilets: None
Contact: (01704) 880587   (Bookings are not necessary)

Travelling Supporters' Information:
Routes: Exit the M6 at Junction 27 and follow signs for Parbold (A5209). After approximately 7 miles turn right into Junction Lane (signposted Burscough/Martin Mere). Turn right at the traffic lights onto the A59 into Burscough Village and pass over canal bridge (2nd left) into Mart Lane for the ground.

GAINSBOROUGH TRINITY FC

Founded: 1873
Former Names: None
Nickname: 'The Blues'
Ground: Northolme, Gainsborough, Lincolnshire, DN21 2QW
Record Attendance: 9,760 (1948)
Pitch Size: 111 × 71 yards

Colours: Blue shirts with White shorts
Telephone No: (01427) 613295 or 614134
Clubhouse Phone No: (01427) 613688
Fax Number: (01427) 613295
Ground Capacity: 4,340
Seating Capacity: 504
Web site: www.gainsboroughtrinity.com

GENERAL INFORMATION

Supporters Club: G. Burton, c/o Club
Telephone No: (01427) 613688
Car Parking: Street parking, in a Local Car Tyre Company car park and also in a Local Authority Car Park nearby
Coach Parking: Opposite the ground
Nearest Railway Station: Lea Road (2 miles)
Nearest Bus Station: Heaton Street (1 mile)
Club Shop: At the ground
Opening Times: Matchdays only
Telephone No: (01427) 611612
Police Telephone No: (01427) 810910

GROUND INFORMATION

Away Supporters' Entrances & Sections:
No usual segregation

ADMISSION INFO (2006/2007 PRICES)

Adult Standing: £8.00
Adult Seating: £9.00
Concessionary Standing: £6.00
Concessionary Seating: £7.00
Under-12s Standing/Seating: £1.00
Children Ages 12 to 16 Standing/Seating: £2.00
Programme Price: £1.50

DISABLED INFORMATION

Wheelchairs: Accommodated
Helpers: Please phone the club for information
Prices: Normal prices for the disabled. Free for helpers
Disabled Toilets: Available in new block adjacent to the Main Stand
Contact: (01427) 613295 (Bookings are not necessary)

Travelling Supporters' Information:
Routes: From the North, South and West: Exit the A1 at Blyth services taking the 1st left through to Bawtry. In Bawtry, turn right at the traffic lights onto the A631 straight through to Gainsborough (approx. 11 miles). Go over the bridge to the second set of traffic lights and turn left onto the A159 (Scunthorpe Road). Follow the main road past Tesco on the right through the traffic lights. The ground is 250 yards on right opposite the Total Petrol station; From the East: Take the A631 into Gainsborough and turn right onto the A159. Then as above.

HARROGATE TOWN FC

Founded: 1919
Former Names: Harrogate FC and Harrogate Hotspurs FC
Nickname: 'Town'
Ground: Wetherby Road, Harrogate   HG2 7SA
Record Attendance: 4,280 (1950)
Pitch Size: 107 × 72 yards

Colours: Yellow and Black striped shirts, Black shorts
Telephone No: (01423) 880675 or 883671
Club Fax Number: (01423) 880675
Ground Capacity: 3,290
Seating Capacity: 502
Web site: www.harrogatetown.com

GENERAL INFORMATION

Supporters Club: c/o Phil Harrison, 14 Chatsworth Grove, Harrogate   HG1 2AS
Telephone/Fax No: (01423) 525211
Car Parking: Hospital Car Park adjacent
Coach Parking: At the ground
Nearest Railway Station: Harrogate (¾ mile)
Nearest Bus Station: Harrogate
Club Shop: At the ground
Opening Times: Matchdays only
Telephone No: (01423) 325111
Police Telephone No: (01423) 505541

GROUND INFORMATION

Away Supporters' Entrances & Sections:
No usual segregation

ADMISSION INFO (2006/2007 PRICES)

Adult Standing: £10.00
Adult Seating: £11.00
Concessionary Standing: £5.00
Concessionary Seating: £6.00
Under-12s Standing: £2.00
Under-12s Seating: £3.00
Programme Price: £2.00

DISABLED INFORMATION

Wheelchairs: Accommodated at the front of the Main Stand
Helpers: Admitted
Prices: Free for the disabled when accompanied by a helper. Normal prices for helpers
Disabled Toilets: Available
Contact: (01423) 880675   (Bookings are not necessary)

Travelling Supporters' Information:
Routes: From the South: Take the A61 from Leeds and turn right at the roundabout onto the ring road (signposted York). After about 1¼ miles turn left at the next roundabout onto A661 Wetherby Road. The ground is situated ¾ mile on the right; From the West: Take the A59 straight into Wetherby Road from Empress Roundabout and the ground is on the left; From the East & North: Exit the A1(M) at Junction 47, take the A59 to Harrogate then follow the Southern bypass to Wetherby Road for the A661 Roundabout. Turn right towards Harrogate Town Centre and the ground is on the right after ¾ mile.

HINCKLEY UNITED FC

Founded: 1889
Former Names: Formed when Hinckley Athletic FC merged with Hinckley Town FC in 1997 (previously Westfield Rovers FC)
Nickname: 'The Knitters'
Ground: Marstons Stadium, Leicester Road, Hinckley, LE10 3DR
Record Attendance: 2,889 (26th December 2006)

Pitch Size: 110 × 72 yards
Colours: Shirts are Blue with Red trim, Blue shorts
Telephone Nº: (01455) 840088
Contact Number: (01455) 840088
Ground Capacity: 4,329
Seating Capacity: 630
Web site: www.hinckleyunitedfc.co.uk

GENERAL INFORMATION
Supporters Club: c/o Club
Telephone Nº: (01455) 840088
Car Parking: At the ground
Coach Parking: At the ground
Nearest Railway Station: Hinckley (2 miles)
Nearest Bus Station: Hinckley
Club Shop: At the ground
Opening Times: Matchdays only
Telephone Nº: (01455) 840088
Police Telephone Nº: (0116) 222-2222

GROUND INFORMATION
Away Supporters' Entrances & Sections:
West Stand and Terrace if required (no usual segregation)

ADMISSION INFO (2007/2008 PRICES)
Adult Standing: £9.00
Adult Seating: £10.00
Under-16s Standing: £3.00
Under-16s Seating: £4.00
Senior Citizen Standing: £6.00
Senior Citizen Seating: £7.00
Programme Price: £2.00

DISABLED INFORMATION
Wheelchairs: Accommodated
Helpers: Admitted
Prices: Normal prices apply
Disabled Toilets: Yes
Contact: (01455) 840088 (Bookings are not necessary)

Travelling Supporters' Information:
Routes: From the North-West: Take the A5 southbound and take the 1st exit at Dodwells roundabout onto the A47 towards Earl Shilton. Go straight on over 3 roundabouts then take the 3rd exit at the next roundabout onto the B4668. The entrance to the ground is on the right after 200 yards; From the South: Take the A5 northbound and upon reaching Dodwells roundabout take the 2nd exit onto the A47 towards East Shilton. Then as above; From the North-East: Take the M69, exit at Junction 2 and follow the B4669 towards Hinckley. After 2 miles (passing through 2 sets of traffic lights) bear right into Spa Lane then turn right at the next set of traffic lights onto the B4668 towards Earl Shilton. The Stadium is on the left after 1¾ miles.

HUCKNALL TOWN FC

Founded: 1946
Former Names: Hucknall Colliery Welfare FC
Nickname: 'The Town'
Ground: Watnall Road, Hucknall, Nottinghamshire, NG15 6EY
Record Attendance: 1,836 (9th April 2005)
Pitch Size: 111 × 72 yards

Colours: Yellow shirts with Black shorts
Social Club Telephone Nº: (0115) 956-1253
Daytime Nº: (0115) 963-0206 (10.00am–4.00pm)
Fax Number: (0115) 963-0716
Ground Capacity: 3,000
Seating Capacity: 500
Web site: www.hucknalltownfc.com

GENERAL INFORMATION

Supporters Club: Mike Drury
Telephone Nº: (0115) 963-0206
Car Parking: Available at the ground
Coach Parking: At the ground
Nearest Railway Station: Hucknall (1 mile)
Nearest Bus Station: Broadmarsh, Nottingham (change for Hucknall)
Club Shop: At the ground
Opening Times: Matchdays or by appointment only
Telephone Nº: (0115) 963-0206
Police Telephone Nº: (0115) 968-0999

GROUND INFORMATION

Away Supporters' Entrances & Sections:
No usual segregation

ADMISSION INFO (2007/2008 PRICES)

Adult Standing: £9.00
Adult Seating: £9.00
Child Standing: £2.00   (Junior Members £1.00)
Child Seating: £2.00   (Junior Members £1.00)
Senior Citizen Standing: £6.00
Senior Citizen Seating: £6.00
Programme Price: £2.00

DISABLED INFORMATION

Wheelchairs: Accommodated
Helpers: Admitted
Prices: Concessionary prices are charged
Disabled Toilets: One available
Contact: (0115) 963-0206   (Bookings are not necessary)

Travelling Supporters' Information:
Routes: Exit the M1 at Junction 27 and take the A608 towards Hucknall. Turn right onto the A611 to Hucknall then take the Hucknall bypass. At the second roundabout join Watnall Road (B6009) and the ground is 100 yards on the right.

HYDE UNITED FC

Founded: 1919
Former Names: Hyde FC (1885-1917)
Nickname: 'Tigers'
Ground: Tameside Stadium, Ewen Fields,
Walker Lane, Hyde, Cheshire   SK14 2SB
Record Attendance: 9,500 (1952)
Pitch Size: 114 × 70 yards
Colours: Red shirts with White shorts

Telephone Nº: 0871 200-2116 (Matchdays) or
07778 792502 (Secretary)
Fax Number: 0871 200-2118 (Ground);
(01270) 212473 (Secretary)
Ground Capacity: 4,250
Seating Capacity: 550
Web site: www.hydeunited.co.uk

GENERAL INFORMATION

Supporters Club: Mark Dring, 16 Gainsborough Walk,
Denton, Manchester   M34 6NS
Telephone Nº: (0161) 336-8076
Car Parking: 150 spaces available at the ground
Coach Parking: At the ground
Nearest Railway Station: Newton (¼ mile)
Nearest Bus Station: Hyde
Club Shop: At the ground
Opening Times: Matchdays only
Telephone Nº: 0871 200-2116
Police Telephone Nº: (0161) 330-8321

GROUND INFORMATION

Away Supporters' Entrances & Sections:
No usual segregation although it is used as required

ADMISSION INFO (2007/2008 PRICES)

Adult Standing: £10.00
Adult Seating: £11.00
Child Standing: £3.00
Child Seating: £4.00
Senior Citizen Standing: £5.00
Senior Citizen Seating: £5.00
Programme Price: £1.50

DISABLED INFORMATION

Wheelchairs: Accommodated in the disabled area
Helpers: Please phone the club for information
Prices: Please phone the club for information
Disabled Toilets: Yes
Contact: (01270) 212473   (Bookings are not necessary)

Travelling Supporters' Information:
Routes: Exit the M60 at Junction 24 and then exit the M67 at Junction 3 for Hyde. Turn right at the top of the slip road, left at the lights (Morrisons on the left). Turn right at the next set of lights into Lumn Road then turn left at the Give Way sign into Walker Lane. Take the 2nd Car Park entrance near the Leisure Pool and follow the road round for the Stadium.

KETTERING TOWN FC

Founded: 1872
Former Names: None
Nickname: 'The Poppies'
Ground: Rockingham Road, Kettering, Northants. NN16 9AW
Record Attendance: 11,526 (1947-48)
Pitch Size: 110 × 70 yards

Colours: Red shirts and shorts
Telephone Nº: (01536) 483028/410815
Daytime Phone Nº: (01536) 483028
Fax Number: (01536) 412273
Ground Capacity: 6,264
Seating Capacity: 1,747
Web site: www.ketteringtownfc.co.uk
E-mail: info@ketteringtownfc.co.uk

GENERAL INFORMATION

Supporters Club: c/o Club
Car Parking: At the ground
Coach Parking: At the 'Beeswing' Public House
Nearest Railway Station: Kettering (1 mile)
Nearest Bus Station: Kettering (1 mile)
Club Shop: At the ground. Also at Elmore's News Shop in Silver Street, Kettering
Opening Times: Shop hours in the Town Centre shop and on request at the ground on Matchdays
Telephone Nº: (01536) 483028
Police Telephone Nº: (01536) 411411

GROUND INFORMATION

Away Supporters' Entrances & Sections:
Rockingham Road End accommodation

ADMISSION INFO (2007/2008 PRICES)

Adult Standing: £10.00
Adult Seating: £12.50
Senior Citizen Standing: £8.00
Senior Citizen Seating: £10.50
Under-16s Standing: £5.00
Under-16s Seating: £5.00
Programme Price: £2.50

DISABLED INFORMATION

Wheelchairs: 12 spaces are available on the terracing adjacent to the Main Stand
Helpers: One helper admitted per wheelchair
Prices: Free of charge for the disabled
Disabled Toilets: Available next to the Social Club
Contact: (01536) 483028 (Bookings are not necessary)

Travelling Supporters' Information:
Routes: To reach Kettering from the A1, M1 or M6, use the A14 to Junction 7, follow the A43 for 1 mile, turn right at the roundabout and the ground is 400 yards on the left on the A6003. (The ground is situated to the North of Kettering (1 mile) on the main A6003 Rockingham Road to Oakham).

LEIGH RMI FC

Founded: 1896
Former Names: Horwich RMI FC
Nickname: 'The Railwaymen'
Ground: Hilton Park, Kirkhall Lane, Leigh, WN7 1RN
Record Attendance: 9,853 (1949)
Pitch Size: 112 × 75 yards

Colours: Red and White shirts with Red shorts
Telephone Nº: (01772) 719266
Fax Number: (01772) 719266
Ground Capacity: 8,500
Seating Capacity: 1,425
Web site: www.leighrmi.com

GENERAL INFORMATION
Supporters Club: c/o Club
Car Parking: 150 spaces available at the ground
Coach Parking: At the ground
Nearest Railway Station: Atherton
Nearest Bus Station: Leigh
Club Shop: At the ground
Opening Times: Daily
Telephone Nº: (01942) 743743
Police Telephone Nº: (01942) 244981

GROUND INFORMATION
Away Supporters' Entrances & Sections:
No usual segregation

ADMISSION INFO (2006/2007 PRICES)
Adult Standing: £10.00
Adult Seating: £10.00
Child/Senior Citizen Standing: £5.00
Child/Senior Citizen Seating: £5.00
Junior Members Standing/Seating: £1.00
Programme Price: £2.00

DISABLED INFORMATION
Wheelchairs: Accommodated by arrangement
Helpers: Admitted
Prices: Normal prices apply
Disabled Toilets: Four available at the ground
Contact: (01772) 719266   (Bookings are not necessary)

Travelling Supporters' Information:
Routes: Exit the M61 at Junction 5 and follow the Westhoughton sign to the roundabout then follow signs for Leigh. Stay on the main road to the traffic lights, turn left into Leigh Road and carry on for about 3 miles until the traffic lights. Turn left and then 1st right at the next set of traffic lights. Turn right onto Atheleigh Way (A579) at the first set of traffic lights and turn left (B & Q on the right), at the next set of traffic lights. Turn right (Leigh Town Centre), at the second opening on the right turn into Prescott Street, carry on to the top, turn right and the ground is on the left.

NUNEATON BOROUGH FC

Ground photograph not available

at the time of going to press

Founded: 1937 (Reformed 1991)
Former Names: Nuneaton Town FC
Nickname: 'Boro'
Ground: Liberty Way, Attleborough Fields Ind. Estate, Nuneaton CV11 6RR
Record Attendance: 22,114 (at Manor Park)
Pitch Size: 121 × 77 yards

Colours: Blue shirts and white shorts
Telephone N°: (024) 7638-5738
Daytime Phone N°: (024) 7638-5738
Fax Number: (024) 7634-2690
Ground Capacity: 6,000
Seating Capacity: 550
Web site: www.nbafc.net

GENERAL INFORMATION
Supporters Club: c/o Liberty Way
Car Parking: Various parking spaces available on the nearby Industria Estate
Coach Parking: At the ground
Nearest Railway Station: Nuneaton (2 miles)
Nearest Bus Station: Nuneaton (2 miles)
Club Shop: Yes – The Boro Shop
Opening Times: Daily from 10.00am to 4.00pm
Telephone N°: (024) 7638-5738
Police Telephone N°: (024) 7664-1111

GROUND INFORMATION
Away Supporters' Entrances & Sections: –

ADMISSION INFO (2007/2008 PRICES)
Adult Standing: £10.00
Adult Seating: £12.00
Concessionary Standing: £6.00
Concessionary Seating: £8.00
Programme Price: £2.00

DISABLED INFORMATION
Wheelchairs: Accommodated
Helpers: Please phone the club for information
Prices: Please phone the club for information
Disabled Toilets: Available
Contact: (024) 7638-5738 (Bookings are necessary)

Travelling Supporters' Information:
Routes: From the South, West and North-West: Exit the M6 at Junction 3 and follow the A444 into Nuneaton. At the Coton Arches roundabout turn right into Avenue Road which is the A4254 signposted for Hinckley. Continue along the A4254 following the road into Garrett Street then Eastboro Way then turn left into Townsend Drive. Follow the road round before turning left into Liberty Way for the ground; From the North: Exit the M1 at Junction 21 and follow the M69. Exit the M69 at Junction 1 and take the 4th exit at the roundabout onto the A5 (Tamworth, Nuneaton). At Longshoot Junction, turn left onto the A47, continue to the roundabout and take the 1st exit onto A4254 Eastborough Way. Turn right at the next roundabout into Townsend Drive then immediately right again for Liberty Way.

REDDITCH UNITED FC

Founded: 1891
Former Names: Redditch Town FC
Nickname: 'The Reds'
Ground: Valley Stadium, Bromsgrove Road, Redditch   B97 4RN
Record Attendance: 5,500 (vs Bromsgrove 1954/55)
Pitch Size: 110 × 72 yards

Colours: Red shirts, shorts and socks
Telephone Nº: (01527) 67450
Contact Nº: (01527) 67450
Fax Number: (01527) 67450
Ground Capacity: 5,000
Seating Capacity: 400
Web site: www.redditchunited.net

GENERAL INFORMATION
Supporters Club: c/o Club
Telephone Nº: (01527) 67450
Car Parking: At the ground
Coach Parking: At the ground
Nearest Railway Station: Redditch (¼ mile)
Nearest Bus Station: Redditch (¼ mile)
Club Shop: None

GROUND INFORMATION
Away Supporters' Entrances & Sections:
No segregation

ADMISSION INFO (2007/2008 PRICES)
Adult Standing: £7.00
Adult Seating: £8.00
Senior Citizen Standing: £5.00
Senior Citizen Seating: £6.00
Under-12s: £2.00 when accompanied by a paying adult
Programme Price: £1.60

DISABLED INFORMATION
Wheelchairs: Accommodated
Helpers: Admitted
Prices: Normal prices apply to both helpers and disabled
Disabled Toilets: Available
Contact: (01527) 67450   (Bookings are not necessary)

Travelling Supporters' Information:
Routes: Exit the M42 at Junction 2 and follow the A441 towards Redditch. Take the 4th exit at the roundabout (signposted Batchley) and turn left at the traffic lights into Birmingham Road. Take the next right into Clive Road then left into Hewell Road. Continue to the T-junction and turn right, passing the Railway Station on the right. Continue through the traffic lights and the ground is situated on the right hand side after about ¼ mile.

SOLIHULL MOORS FC

Founded: 2007
Former Names: Formed by the merger of Solihull Borough FC and Moor Green FC in 2007
Nickname: 'The Moors'
Ground: Damson Park, Damson Parkway, Solihull, B91 2PP
Record Attendance: 2,000 (vs Birmingham City)

Pitch Size: 110 × 75 yards
Colours: Red shirts with White shorts
Telephone Nº: (0121) 705-6770
Fax Number: (0121) 711-4045
Ground Capacity: 3,050
Seating Capacity: 280
Web site: www.solihullmoorsfc.co.uk

GENERAL INFORMATION
Supporters Club: –
Car Parking: At the ground
Coach Parking: At the ground
Nearest Railway Station: Birmingham International (2 miles)
Nearest Bus Station: Birmingham (5 miles)
Club Shop: At the ground
Opening Times: Matchdays only
Telephone Nº: (0121) 705-6770
Police Telephone Nº: (0121) 706-8111

GROUND INFORMATION
Away Supporters' Entrances & Sections:
No usual segregation

ADMISSION INFO (2007/2008 PRICES)
Adult Standing: £9.00
Adult Seating: £9.00
Senior Citizen/Junior Standing: £4.00
Senior Citizen/Junior Seating: £4.00
Under-16s: Free of charge with a paying adult
Programme Price: £1.50

DISABLED INFORMATION
Wheelchairs: Spaces for 3 wheelchairs are available
Helpers: Admitted
Prices: Normal prices apply
Disabled Toilets: Available
Contact: (0121) 705-6770

Travelling Supporters' Information:
Routes: Exit the M42 at Junction 6 and take the A45 for 2 miles towards Birmingham. Turn left at the traffic lights near the Posthouse Hotel into Damson Parkway (signposted for Landrover/Damsonwood). Continue to the roundabout and come back along the other carriageway to the ground which is situated on the left after about 150 yards.

SOUTHPORT FC

Founded: 1881
Former Names: Southport Vulcan FC, Southport Central FC
Nickname: 'The Sandgrounders'
Ground: Haig Avenue, Southport, Merseyside, PR8 6JZ
Record Attendance: 20,010 (1932)
Pitch Size: 110 × 77 yards

Colours: Yellow shirts with Black shorts
Telephone Nº: (01704) 533422
Fax Number: (01704) 533455
Ground Capacity: 6,001
Seating Capacity: 1,640
Web site: www.southportfc.net

GENERAL INFORMATION

Supporters Club: Grandstand Club
Telephone Nº: (01704) 530182
Car Parking: Street parking
Coach Parking: Adjacent to the ground
Nearest Railway Station: Southport (1½ miles)
Nearest Bus Station: Southport Town Centre
Club Shop: At the ground
Opening Times: Matchdays from 1.30pm (or 6.30pm for evening matches); Fridays 4.30pm to 6.30pm
Telephone Nº: (01704) 533422
Police Telephone Nº: (0151) 709-6010

GROUND INFORMATION

Away Supporters' Entrances & Sections:
Blowick End entrances

ADMISSION INFO (2007/2008 PRICES)

Adult Standing: £11.00
Adult Seating: £12.50
Child/Senior Citizen Standing: £7.50
Child/Senior Citizen Seating: £8.50
Programme Price: £2.50

DISABLED INFORMATION

Wheelchairs: Accommodated in front of the Grandstand
Helpers: Admitted
Prices: Concessionary prices charged for the disabled. Helpers are admitted free of charge
Disabled Toilets: Available at the Blowick End of the Grandstand
Contact: (01704) 533422 (Bookings are not necessary)

Travelling Supporters' Information:
Routes: Exit the M58 at Junction 3 and take the A570 to Southport. At the major roundabout (McDonalds/Tesco) go straight on into Scarisbrick New Road, pass over the brook and turn right into Haig Avenue at the traffic lights. The ground is then on the right-hand side.

STALYBRIDGE CELTIC FC

Founded: 1909
Former Names: None
Nickname: 'Celtic'
Ground: Bower Fold, Mottram Road, Stalybridge,
Cheshire SK15 2RT
Record Attendance: 9,753 (1922/23)
Pitch Size: 109 × 70 yards

Colours: Blue shirts, shorts and socks
Telephone Nº: (0161) 338-2828
Daytime Phone Nº: (0161) 338-2828
Fax Number: (0161) 338-8256
Ground Capacity: 6,108
Seating Capacity: 1,155
Web site: www.stalybridgeceltic.co.uk

GENERAL INFORMATION

Supporters Club: Bob Rhodes, c/o Club
Telephone Nº: (01457) 764044
Car Parking: At the ground
Coach Parking: At the ground
Nearest Railway Station: Stalybridge (1 mile)
Nearest Bus Station: Stalybridge town centre
Club Shop: At the ground
Opening Times: Matchdays only
Telephone Nº: (0161) 338-2828
Police Telephone Nº: (0161) 330-8321

GROUND INFORMATION

Away Supporters' Entrances & Sections:
Lockwood & Greenwood Stand

ADMISSION INFO (2007/2008 PRICES)

Adult Standing: £10.00
Adult Seating: £10.00
Under-14s Standing/Seating: Free of charge
Concessionary Standing: £6.00
Concessionary Seating: £6.00
Programme Price: £2.00

DISABLED INFORMATION

Wheelchairs: 20 spaces available each for home and away
fans at the side of the Stepan Stand. A further 9 spaces
available in the new Lord Tom Pendry Stand
Helpers: Please phone the club for information
Prices: Please phone the club for information
Disabled Toilets: Available at the rear of the Stepan Stand
and at the side of the Lord Tom Pendry Stand
Contact: (0161) 338-2828 (Bookings are necessary)

Travelling Supporters' Information:
Routes: From the Midlands and South: Take the M6, M56, M60 and M67, leaving at the end of the motorway. Go across the
roundabout to the traffic lights and turn left. The ground is approximately 2 miles on the left before the Hare & Hounds pub; From
the North: Exit the M62 at Junction 18 onto the M60 singposted for Ashton-under-Lyne. Follow the M60 to Junction 24 and
join the M67, then as from the Midlands and South.

TAMWORTH FC

Founded: 1933
Former Names: None
Nickname: 'The Lambs'
Ground: The Lamb Ground, Kettlebrook, Tamworth, B77 1AA
Record Attendance: 4,920 (3/4/48)
Pitch Size: 110 × 73 yards

Colours: Red shirts and shorts
Telephone Nº: (01827) 65798
Daytime Phone Nº: (01827) 65798
Fax Number: (01827) 62236
Ground Capacity: 4,118
Seating Capacity: 520
Web site: www.thelambs.co.uk

GENERAL INFORMATION

Supporters Club: Dave Clayton, c/o Club
Telephone Nº: (0781) 5046899
Car Parking: 200 spaces available at the ground – £1.00 per car or £10.00 per coach
Coach Parking: At the ground
Nearest Railway Station: Tamworth (½ mile)
Nearest Bus Station: Tamworth (½ mile)
Club Shop: At the ground
Opening Times: Weekdays & Matchdays 10.00am – 4.00pm
Telephone Nº: (01827) 65798
Police Telephone Nº: (01827) 61001

GROUND INFORMATION

Away Supporters' Entrances & Sections:
Gates 1 and 2 for Terracing, Gate 2A for seating

ADMISSION INFO (2007/2008 PRICES)

Adult Standing: £11.00
Adult Seating: £13.00
Child/Senior Citizen Standing: £6.00
Child/Senior Citizen Seating: £9.00
Programme Price: £2.00

DISABLED INFORMATION

Wheelchairs: Accommodated
Helpers: Admitted
Prices: Normal prices apply for Wheelchair disabled. Helpers are charged concessionary rates
Disabled Toilets: Yes
Contact: (01827) 65798   (Bookings are advisable)

Travelling Supporters' Information:
Routes: Exit the M42 at Junction 10 and take the A5/A51 to the town centre following signs for Town Centre/Snowdome. The follow signs for Kettlebrook and the ground is in Kettlebrook Road, 50 yards from the traffic island by the Railway Viaduct and the Snowdome. The ground is signposted from all major roads.

VAUXHALL MOTORS FC

Founded: 1963
Former Names: Vauxhall GM FC
Nickname: 'Motormen'
Ground: Rivacre Park, Hooton, Ellesmere Port, Cheshire   CH66 1NJ
Record Attendance: 1,500 (1987)
Pitch Size: 110 × 70 yards
Colours: White shirts with Dark Blue shorts

Telephone Nº: (0151) 328-1114 (Ground)
Ground Capacity: 2,500
Seating Capacity: 266
Contact: Carole Paisey, 31 South Road, West Kirby, Wirral   CH48 3HG
Contact Phone and Fax Nº: (0151) 625-6936
Web site: www.vmfc.com
E-mail: office@vmfc.com

GENERAL INFORMATION
Supporters Club: At the ground
Telephone/Fax Nº: (0151) 328-1114
Car Parking: At the ground
Coach Parking: At the ground
Nearest Railway Station: Hooton
Nearest Bus Station: Ellesmere Port
Club Shop: At the ground
Opening Times: Matchdays only
Telephone Nº: –

GROUND INFORMATION
Away Supporters' Entrances & Sections:
No usual segregation

ADMISSION INFO (2006/2007 PRICES)
Adult Standing/Seating: £8.00
Child Standing/Seating: £3.00
Senior Citizen Standing/Seating: £5.00
Programme Price: £2.00

DISABLED INFORMATION
Wheelchairs: Accommodated as necessary
Helpers: Admitted
Prices: Normal prices for the disabled. Free for helpers
Disabled Toilets: Available
Contact: –   (Bookings are not necessary)

Travelling Supporters' Information:
Routes: Exit the M53 at Junction 5 and take the A41 towards Chester. Turn left at the first set of traffic lights into Hooton Green. Turn left at the first T-junction then right at the next T-junction into Rivacre Road. The ground is situated 250 yards on the right.

WORCESTER CITY FC

Founded: 1902
Former Names: Berwick Rangers FC
Nickname: 'The City'
Ground: St. Georges Lane, Worcester WR1 1QT
Record Attendance: 17,042 (1958/59)
Pitch Size: 110 × 75 yards

Colours: Blue and White shirts with Black shorts
Telephone Nº: (01905) 23003
Fax Number: (01905) 26668
Ground Capacity: 4,500
Seating Capacity: 1,100
Web site: www.worcestercityfc.co.uk

GENERAL INFORMATION

Supporters Club: P. Gardner, c/o Club
Telephone Nº: –
Car Parking: Street parking
Coach Parking: Street parking
Nearest Railway Station: Foregate Street (1 mile)
Nearest Bus Station: Crowngate Bus Station
Club Shop: At the ground
Opening Times: Matchdays only 10.00am – 5.00pm
Telephone Nº: (01905) 23003
Police Telephone Nº: (01905) 723888

GROUND INFORMATION

Away Supporters' Entrances & Sections:
Turnstile at the Canal End when segregation in in force for
Canal End accommodation

ADMISSION INFO (2007/2008 PRICES)

Adult Standing: £10.00
Adult Seating: £11.00
Child/Senior Citizen Standing: £5.00
Child/Senior Citizen Seating: £6.00
Programme Price: £2.00

DISABLED INFORMATION

Wheelchairs: 3 covered spaces available
Helpers: Please phone the club for information
Prices: Please phone the club for information
Disabled Toilets: None
Contact: (01905) 23003 (Bookings are necessary)

Travelling Supporters' Information:
Routes: Exit the M5 at Junction 6 and take the A449 Kidderminster Road. Follow to the end of the dual carriageway and take
the second exit at the roundabout for Worcester City Centre. At the first set of traffic lights turn right into the town centre. The
3rd turning on the left is St. Georges Lane.

WORKINGTON AFC

Founded: 1884 (Reformed 1921)
Former Names: None
Nickname: 'Reds'
Ground: Borough Park, Workington   CA14 2DT
Record Attendance: 21,000 (vs Manchester United)
Pitch Size: 110 × 71 yards

Colours: Red shirts and shorts
Telephone Nº: (01900) 602871
Fax Number: (01900) 67432
Ground Capacity: 3,100
Seating Capacity: 500
Web site: www.workingtonafc.co.uk

GENERAL INFORMATION
Supporters Club: Yes
Car Parking: Car Park next to the ground
Coach Parking: At the ground
Nearest Railway Station: Workington (¼ mile)
Nearest Bus Station: Workington (½ mile)
Club Shop: At the ground
Opening Times: Matchdays only
Telephone Nº: (01946) 832710

GROUND INFORMATION
Away Supporters' Entrances & Sections:
No usual segregation

ADMISSION INFO (2007/2008 PRICES)
Adult Standing: £10.00
Adult Seating: £10.00
Senior Citizen/Junior Standing: £5.00
Senior Citizen/Junior Seating: £5.00
Programme Price: £1.80

DISABLED INFORMATION
Wheelchairs: Accommodated
Helpers: Admitted
Prices: Normal prices apply
Disabled Toilets: Available
Contact: (01900) 602871   (Bookings are not necessary)

Travelling Supporters' Information:
Routes: Exit the M6 at Junction 40 and take the A66 towards Keswick and Workington. Upon reaching Workington, continue until you reach the traffic lights at a T-junction. Turn right here onto the A596 for Maryport. After approximately ½ mile you will see the ground floodlights on the opposite site of the river (to the left). Continue along the A596, pass under the bridge taking the next right signposted for the Stadium. The ground is then on the left hand side opposite the Tesco superstore.

THE FOOTBALL CONFERENCE BLUE SQUARE SOUTH

Address

Riverside House, 14B High Street,
Crayford, Kent   DA1 4HG

Phone (01322) 411021   **Fax** (01322) 411022

Web site   www.footballconference.co.uk

Clubs for the 2007/2008 Season

BASINGSTOKE TOWN FC

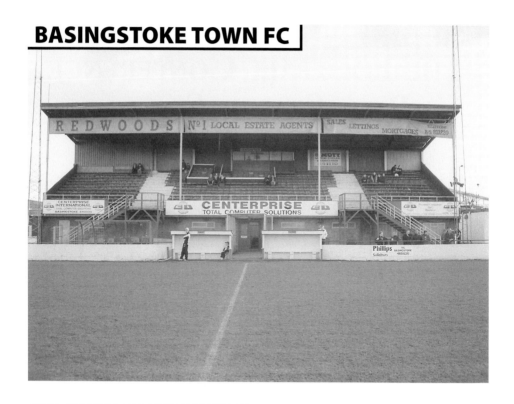

Founded: 1896
Former Names: None
Nickname: 'Dragons'
Ground: The Camrose Ground, Western Way, Basingstoke, Hants. RG22 6EZ
Record Attendance: 5,085 (25/11/97)
Pitch Size: 110 × 70 yards

Colours: Yellow and Blue shirts with Blue shorts
Telephone Nº: (01256) 327575
Fax Number: (01256) 869997
Social Club Nº: (01256) 464353
Ground Capacity: 6,000
Seating Capacity: 650
Web site: www.btfc.co.uk

GENERAL INFORMATION

Supporters Club: c/o Club
Telephone Nº: (01256) 327575
Car Parking: 600 spaces available at the ground
Coach Parking: Ample room available at ground
Nearest Railway Station: Basingstoke
Nearest Bus Station: Basingstoke Town Centre (2 miles)
Club Shop: The Camrose Shop
Opening Times: Matchdays only
Telephone Nº: (01256) 327575
Police Telephone Nº: (01256) 473111

GROUND INFORMATION

Away Supporters' Entrances & Sections:
No usual segregation

ADMISSION INFO (2007/2008 PRICES)

Adult Standing: £10.00
Adult Seating: £11.00
Concessionary Standing: £6.00
Concessionary Seating: £7.00
Under-16s Standing: £3.00
Under-16s Seating: £4.00
Programme Price: £2.00

DISABLED INFORMATION

Wheelchairs: 6 spaces are available under cover
Helpers: Admitted
Prices: Normal prices for the disabled. Free for helpers
Disabled Toilets: Yes
Contact: (01256) 327575 (Bookings are not necessary)

Travelling Supporters' Information:
Routes: Exit the M3 at Junction 6 and take the 1st left at the Black Dam roundabout. At the next roundabout take the 2nd exit, then the 1st exit at the following roundabout and the 5th exit at the next roundabout. This takes you into Western Way and the ground is 50 yards on the right.

BATH CITY FC

Founded: 1889
Former Names: Bath AFC, Bath Railway FC and Bath Amateurs FC
Nickname: 'The Romans'
Ground: Twerton Park, Bath   BA2 1DB
Record Attendance: 18,020 (1960)
Pitch Size: 110 × 76 yards

Colours: Black and White striped shirts, Black shorts
Telephone Nº: (01225) 423087/313247
Fax Number: (01225) 481391
Ground Capacity: 8,840
Seating Capacity: 1,026
Web site: www.bathcityfc.com

GENERAL INFORMATION

Supporters Club: Martin Brush, c/o Club
Telephone Nº: (01225) 423087
Car Parking: 150 spaces available at the ground
Coach Parking: Available at the ground
Nearest Railway Station: Bath Spa (1½ miles)
Nearest Bus Station: Avon Street, Bath
Club Shop: Yes – contact Martin Brush, c/o Club
Opening Times: Matchdays and office hours
Telephone Nº: (01225) 423087

GROUND INFORMATION

Away Supporters' Entrances & Sections:
No usual segregation

ADMISSION INFO (2007/2008 PRICES)

Adult Standing: £9.50
Adult Seating: £11.00
Senior Citizen Standing: £6.00
Senior Citizen Seating: £7.50
Under-16s Standing: £3.50
Under-16s Seating: £4.50
Programme Price: £1.50

DISABLED INFORMATION

Wheelchairs: 10 spaces available each for home and away fans in front of the Family Stand
Helpers: Admitted
Prices: £6.00 or £9.50 for disabled. Free entrance for helpers
Disabled Toilets: Available behind the Family Stand
Contact: (01225) 423087   (Bookings are not necessary)

Travelling Supporters' Information:
Route: As a recommendation, avoid exiting the M4 at Junction 18 as the road from takes you through Bath City Centre. Instead, exit the M4 at Junction 19 onto the M32. Turn off the M32 at Junction 1 and follow the A4174 Bristol Ring Road south then join the A4 for Bath. On the A4, after passing through Saltford you will reach a roundabout shortly before entering Bath. Take the 2nd exit at this roundabout then follow the road before turning left into Newton Road at the bottom of the steep hill. The ground is then on the right hand side of the road.

BISHOP'S STORTFORD FC

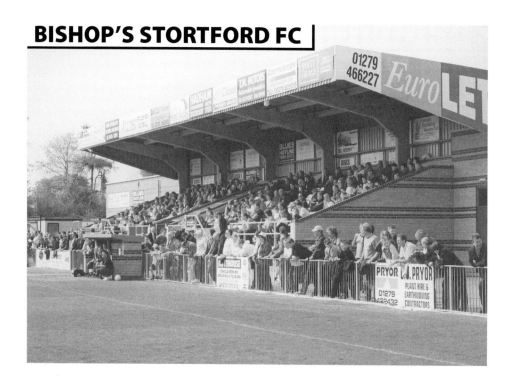

Founded: 1874
Former Names: None
Nickname: 'Blues' 'Bishops'
Ground: Woodside Park, Dunmow Road,
Bishop's Stortford CM23 5RG
Record Attendance: 3,555 (2000)
Pitch Size: 110 × 70 yards

Colours: Blue and White shirts with Blue shorts
Telephone N°: (08700) 339930
Fax Number: (08700) 339931
Ground Capacity: 4,000
Seating Capacity: 500
Web site: www.bsfc.co.uk

GENERAL INFORMATION

Supporters Club: None
Car Parking: 150 spaces available at the ground
Coach Parking: At the ground
Nearest Railway Station: Bishop's Stortford
Nearest Bus Station: Bishop's Stortford
Club Shop: At the ground
Opening Times: Matchdays only 1.30pm to 5.00pm
Telephone N°: (08700) 339930
Police Telephone N°: –

GROUND INFORMATION

Away Supporters' Entrances & Sections:
No usual segregation

ADMISSION INFO (2007/2008 PRICES)

Adult Standing: £10.00
Adult Seating: £10.00
Child Standing: £5.00
Child Seating: £5.00
Programme Price: £2.00

DISABLED INFORMATION

Wheelchairs: Accommodated in the disabled section
Helpers: Admitted
Prices: Free of charge for the disabled and helpers
Disabled Toilets: Yes
Contact: (08700) 339930 (Bookings are not necessary)

Travelling Supporters' Information:
Routes: Exit the M11 at junction 8 and take the A1250 towards Bishop Stortford. Turn left at the first roundabout and the ground is first right opposite the Golf Club (the entrance is between Industrial Units).

BOGNOR REGIS TOWN FC

Founded: 1883
Former Names: None
Nickname: 'The Rocks'
Ground: Nyewood Lane, Bognor Regis   PO21 2TY
Record Attendance: 3,642 (1984)
Pitch Size: 116 × 75 yards

Colours: White shirts with Green trim, Green shorts
Telephone Nº: (01243) 822325
Fax Number: (01243) 866151
Ground Capacity: 6,000
Seating Capacity: 243
Web site: www.therocks.co.uk

GENERAL INFORMATION

Supporters Club: David Seabourne, c/o Club
Telephone Nº: (01243) 861336
Car Parking: Outside the ground at the Sports Club
Coach Parking: None
Nearest Railway Station: Bognor Regis (1 mile)
Nearest Bus Station: Bognor Regis (1 mile)
Club Shop: At the ground
Opening Times: Matchdays only
Telephone Nº: (01243) 862045
Police Telephone Nº: (0845) 607-0999

GROUND INFORMATION

Away Supporters' Entrances & Sections:
No usual segregation

ADMISSION INFO (2007/2008 PRICES)

Adult Standing: £9.00
Adult Seating: £10.00
Senior Citizen Standing: £6.00
Senior Citizen Seating: £7.00
Child Standing: £2.00
Child Seating: £3.00
Programme Price: £1.50

DISABLED INFORMATION

Wheelchairs: Accommodated
Helpers: Admitted
Prices: Normal prices apply
Disabled Toilets: Available
Contact: (01243) 822325   (Bookings are not necessary)

Travelling Supporters' Information:
Routes: From the West: Take the M27/A27 to Chichester then the A259 and pass through Bersted towards Bognor Regis. Turn right into Hawthorne Road then left into Nyewood Lane – the ground is on the right; From the East: Take the A27 from Brighton/Worthing and turn left onto the A29 at Fontwell Roundabout past Denmans Garden Centre. Travel along Shripney Road and turn right at the second roundabout towards Bersted on the A259 then left into Hawthorne Road – then as above.

BRAINTREE TOWN FC

Founded: 1898
Former Names: Manor Works FC, Crittall Athletic FC, Braintree & Crittall Athletic FC and Braintree FC
Nickname: 'The Iron'
Ground: Cressing Road Stadium, Clockhouse Way, Braintree, Essex   CM7 6RD
Record Attendance: 4,000 (May 1952)
Pitch Size: 110 × 70 yards

Ground Capacity: 3,400
Seating Capacity: 284
Colours: Yellow shirts and socks
Telephone Nº: (01376) 345617
Fax Number: (01376) 330976
Correspondence Address: Tom Woodley, 19A Bailey Bridge Road, Braintree   CM7 5TT
Contact Telephone Nº: (01376) 326234
Web site: www.braintreetownfc.org.uk

GENERAL INFORMATION
Supporters Club: c/o Club
Telephone Nº: (01376) 345617
Car Parking: At the ground
Coach Parking: At the ground
Nearest Railway Station: Braintree & Bocking (1 mile)
Nearest Bus Station: Braintree
Club Shop: At the ground
Opening Times: Matchdays only
Telephone Nº: (01376) 345617

GROUND INFORMATION
Away Supporters' Entrances & Sections:
No usual segregation

ADMISSION INFO (2007/2008 PRICES)
Adult Standing: £10.00
Adult Seating: £10.00
Child Standing: £5.00
Child Seating: £5.00
Programme Price: £2.00

DISABLED INFORMATION
Wheelchairs: Accommodated
Helpers: Admitted
Prices: Normal prices apply
Disabled Toilets: Available
Contact: –   (Bookings are not necessary)

Travelling Supporters' Information:
Routes: Exit the A120 Braintree Bypass at the McDonald's roundabout following signs for East Braintree Industrial Estate. The floodlights at the ground are visible on the left ½ mile into town. Turn left into Clockhouse Way then left again for the ground.

BROMLEY FC

Founded: 1892
Former Names: None
Nickname: 'Lillywhites'
Ground: The Stadium, Hayes Lane, Bromley, Kent, BR2 9EF
Record Attendance: 12,000 (24/9/49)
Pitch Size: 112 × 72 yards

Colours: White shirts with Black shorts
Telephone Nº: (020) 8460-5291
Fax Number: –
Ground Capacity: 3,300
Seating Capacity: 1,300
Web site: www.bromleyfc.net

GENERAL INFORMATION

Car Parking: 300 spaces available at the ground
Coach Parking: At the ground
Nearest Railway Station: Bromley South (1 mile)
Nearest Bus Station: High Street, Bromley
Club Shop: At the ground
Opening Times: Matchdays only
Telephone Nº: (020) 8460-5291

GROUND INFORMATION

Away Supporters' Entrances & Sections:
No usual segregation

ADMISSION INFO (2007/2008 PRICES)

Adult Standing: £10.00
Adult Seating: £10.00
Child/Senior Citizen Standing: £5.00
Child/Senior Citizen Seating: £5.00
Note: Each 2nd child with a paying adult is admitted for free
Programme Price: £2.00

DISABLED INFORMATION

Wheelchairs: Accommodated
Helpers: Admitted
Prices: Please phone the club for information
Disabled Toilets: Yes
Contact: (0181) 460-5291   (Bookings are necessary)

Travelling Supporters' Information:
Routes: Exit the M25 at Junction 4 and follow the A21 for Bromley and London for approximately 4 miles before forking left onto the A232 signposted for Croydon/Sutton. At the second set of traffic lights turn left into Baston Road (B265) and follow for approximately 2 miles as it become Hayes Street and then Hayes Lane. The ground is on the right just after a mini-roundabout.

CAMBRIDGE CITY FC

Founded: 1908
Former Names: Cambridge Town FC
Nickname: 'Lilywhites'
Ground: City Ground, Milton Road, Cambridge, CB4 1UY
Record Attendance: 12,058 (1950)
Pitch Size: 110 × 70 yards

Colours: White shirts with Black shorts
Telephone Nº: (01223) 357973
Fax Number: (01223) 351582
Ground Capacity: 3,000
Seating Capacity: 523
Correspondence: Kevin Peters, 9 Villa Court, Cambridge CB4 2TX
Web site: www.cambridgecityfc.com

GENERAL INFORMATION

Supporters Trust: Terry Dunn, c/o Club
Telephone Nº: (01223) 357973
Car Parking: 300 spaces available at the ground
Coach Parking: At the ground
Nearest Railway Station: Cambridge (2 miles)
Nearest Bus Station: Cambridge
Club Shop: At the ground
Opening Times: Matchdays only
Telephone Nº: (01223) 357973
Police Telephone Nº: (01223) 358966

GROUND INFORMATION

Away Supporters' Entrances & Sections:
No usual segregation

ADMISSION INFO (2007/2008 PRICES)

Adult Standing: £10.00
Adult Seating: £10.00
Senior Citizen/Under-16s Standing: £5.00
Senior Citizen/Under-16s Seating: £5.00
Under-12s Standing/Seating: £2.00
Family Ticket: 2 adults + 3 children £17.00
Programme Price: £2.00

DISABLED INFORMATION

Wheelchairs: 6 spaces are available under cover on the half-way line
Helpers: Admitted
Prices: Free of charge for the disabled. One helper admitted free with each disabled fan
Disabled Toilets: One available in the Main Stand
Contact: (01223) 357973 (Bookings are not necessary)

Travelling Supporters' Information:
Routes: Exit the M11 at Junction 13 and take the A1303 into the City. At the end of Madingley Road, turn left into Chesterton Lane and then Chesterton Road. Go into the one-way system and turn left into Milton Road (A10) and the ground is on the left behind the Westbrook Centre.

DORCHESTER TOWN FC

Founded: 1880
Former Names: None
Nickname: 'The Magpies'
Ground: The Avenue Stadium, Weymouth Avenue, Dorchester, Dorset DT1 2RY
Record Attendance: 4,159 (1/1/99)
Pitch Size: 110 × 80 yards

Colours: Black & White striped shirts, Black shorts
Telephone Nº: (01305) 262451
Daytime Nº: (01305) 262451 or 262527
Fax Number: (01305) 267623
Ground Capacity: 5,009
Seating Capacity: 710
Web Site: www.the-magpies.net

GENERAL INFORMATION

Supporters Club: H.G. Hill, 39 Thatcham Park, Yeovil, Somerset
Telephone Nº: (01935) 422536
Car Parking: 350 spaces available at the ground (£1.00 fee)
Coach Parking: At the ground
Nearest Railway Station: Dorchester South and West (both 1 mile)
Nearest Bus Station: Nearby
Club Shop: At the ground
Opening Times: During 1st team matchdays only
Telephone Nº: (01305) 262451
Police Telephone Nº: (01305) 251212

GROUND INFORMATION

Away Supporters' Entrances & Sections:
Main Stand side when segregated (not usual)

ADMISSION INFO (2007/2008 PRICES)

Adult Standing: £9.00
Adult Seating: £10.00
Senior Citizen/Child Standing: £5.50
Senior Citizen/Child Seating: £6.50
Under-16s: £2.50 when accompanied by a paying adult
Programme Price: £2.00

DISABLED INFORMATION

Wheelchairs: 10 spaces available each for home and away fans at the North West End of the terracing
Helpers: Admitted
Prices: Normal prices apply
Disabled Toilets: 2 available near the disabled area
Contact: (01305) 262451 (Bookings are not necessary)

Travelling Supporters' Information:
Routes: Take the Dorchester Bypass (A35) from all directions. The ground is on the South side of town, adjacent to a roundabout at the intersection with the A354 to Weymouth. Alternatively, take Weymouth signs from Dorchester Town Centre for 1½ miles.

EASTBOURNE BOROUGH FC

Founded: 1963
Former Names: Langney Sports FC
Nickname: 'The Sports'
Ground: Priory Lane Stadium, Langney Sports Club, Priory Lane, Eastbourne   BN23 7QH
Record Attendance: 3,770 (5th November 2005)
Pitch Size: 115 × 72 yards

Colours: Red shirts with Black shorts
Telephone Nº: (01323) 743561
Fax Number: (01323) 741627
Ground Capacity: 5,644
Seating Capacity: 542
Web site: www.eastbourneboroughfc.co.uk

GENERAL INFORMATION
Supporters Club: Yes – c/o Club
Telephone Nº: –
Car Parking: Around 400 spaces available at the ground
Coach Parking: At the ground
Nearest Railway Station: Pevensey & Westham (1½ miles but no public transport to the ground)
Nearest Bus Station: Eastbourne
Club Shop: At the ground
Opening Times: Matchdays only
Telephone Nº: (01323) 743561
Police Telephone Nº: (0845) 607-0999

GROUND INFORMATION
Away Supporters' Entrances & Sections:
No usual segregation

ADMISSION INFO (2007/2008 PRICES)
Adult Standing: £9.50
Adult Seating: £9.50
Child Standing: £2.50 (Under-16s)
Child Seating: £2.50 (Under-16s)
Senior Citizen Standing: £6.00
Senior Citizen Seating: £6.00
Programme Price: £2.00

DISABLED INFORMATION
Wheelchairs: 6 spaces available
Helpers: Admitted
Prices: Normal prices apply
Disabled Toilets: Available
Contact: (01323) 743561   (Bookings are not necessary)

Travelling Supporters' Information:
Routes: Approaching from the A22: Take the first exit to join the Polegate bypass, signposted A27 Eastbourne, Hastings & Bexhill. *Take the 2nd exit at the next roundabout for Stone Cross and Westham (A22) then the first exit at the following roundabout signposted Stone Cross and Westham. Turn right after ½ mile into Friday Street (B2104). At the end of Friday Street, turn left at the double mini-roundabout into Hide Hollow (B2191), passing Eastbourne Crematorium on your right. Turn right at the roundabout into Priory Road, and Priory Lane is about 200 yards down the road on the left; Approaching from the A27 from Brighton: Turn left at the Polegate traffic lights then take 2nd exit at the large roundabout to join the bypass. Then as from *.

EASTLEIGH FC

Photo courtesy of the Southern Daily Echo

Founded: 1946
Former Names: Swathing Athletic FC, Swathing FC
Nickname: 'The Spitfires'
Ground: Silverlake Stadium, Ten Acres, Stoneham Lane, Eastleigh   SO50 9HT
Record Attendance: 3,104 (1976)
Pitch Size: 110 × 70 yards

Colours: White shirts with Blue shorts
Telephone N°: (023) 8061-3361
Fax Number: (023) 8061-2379
Ground Capacity: 3,500
Seating Capacity: 350
Web site: www.eastleigh-fc.co.uk
e-mail: commercial@eastleigh-fc.co.uk

GENERAL INFORMATION

Car Parking: Spaces for 450 cars available (hard standing)
Coach Parking: At the ground
Nearest Railway Station: Southampton Parkway (¾ mile)
Nearest Bus Station: Eastleigh (2 miles)
Club Shop: At the ground
Opening Times: Matchdays and during functions only

GROUND INFORMATION

Away Supporters' Entrances & Sections:
No usual segregation

ADMISSION INFO (2007/2008 PRICES)

Adult Standing/Seating: £10.00
Senior Citizen Standing/Seating: £6.00
Ages 16 to 18 Standing/Seating: £3.00
Ages 12 to 16 Standing/Seating: £1.00
Under-12s: Free of charge
Programme Price: £2.00

DISABLED INFORMATION

Wheelchairs: Accommodated
Helpers: Admitted
Prices: Normal prices apply
Disabled Toilets: Available
Contact: (023) 8061-3361   (Bookings are not necessary)

Travelling Supporters' Information:
Routes: Exit the M27 at Junction 5 (signposted for Southampton Airport) and take the A335 (Stoneham Way) towards Southampton. After ½ mile, turn right at the traffic lights into Bassett Green Road. Turn right at the next set of traffic lights into Stoneham Lane and the ground is on the right after ¾ mile.

FISHER ATHLETIC (LONDON) FC

The club are currently groundsharing with Dulwich Hamlet FC.

Founded: 1908
Former Names: Fisher Athletic FC, Fisher '93 FC
Nickname: 'The Fish'
Ground: Champion Hill Stadium, Edgar Kail Way, London SE22 8BD
Record Attendance: 4,283 (vs Barnet 4/5/1991)
Pitch Size: 110 × 70 yards

Colours: Black and White striped shirts, White shorts
Telephone Nº: (020) 7326-1360
Fax Number: (020) 7326-0163
Ground Capacity: 3,000
Seating Capacity: 500
Web site: www.fisherathletic.co.uk

GENERAL INFORMATION

Supporters Club: None
Telephone Nº: –
Car Parking: 50 spaces available at the ground
Coach Parking: At the ground
Nearest Railway Station: East Dulwich (adjacent)
Nearest Bus Station: East Dulwich
Club Shop: At the ground
Opening Times: Matchdays only
Telephone Nº: (020) 7231-5144
Police Telephone Nº: (020) 8693-3366

GROUND INFORMATION

Away Supporters' Entrances & Sections:
No usual segregation

ADMISSION INFO (2007/2008 PRICES)

Adult Standing: £9.00
Adult Seating: £9.00
Concessionary Standing: £5.00
Concessionary Seating: £5.00
Ages 12 to 16 Standing/Seating: £2.00
Under-12s: Free of charge
Programme Price: £1.50

DISABLED INFORMATION

Wheelchairs: Accommodated
Helpers: Please phone the club for information
Prices: Please phone the club for information
Disabled Toilets: Available
Contact: (020) 7231-5144   (Bookings are not necessary)

Travelling Supporters' Information:
Routes: From the Elephant & Castle: Go down Walworth Road, through Camberwell's one-way system and along Denmark Hill. Turn left by the railway into Champion Park and then right at the end down Grave Lane to the ground in Dog Kennel Hill; From the South: Come up through Streatham on the A23, turn right to Tulse Hill along the A205 (Christchurch Road) and carry on towards Sydenham. Turn left at The Grove into Lordship Lane and carry on to East Dulwich.

HAMPTON & RICHMOND BOROUGH FC

Founded: 1921
Former Names: Hampton FC
Nickname: 'Beavers'
Ground: Beveree Stadium, Beaver Close,
off Station Road, Hampton, Middlesex   TW12 2BX
Record Attendance: 2,250 vs AFC Wimbledon
Pitch Size: 113 × 71 yards

Colours: Red shirts with Blue shorts
Matchday Phone Nº: (020) 8979-2456
Fax Number: (020) 8979-2456
Ground Capacity: 3,300
Seating Capacity: 300
Web site: www.hamptonfc.com

GENERAL INFORMATION
Supporters Club: Yes
Telephone Nº: (07968) 778761
Car Parking: At the ground and street parking
Coach Parking: Contact the Club for information
Nearest Railway Station: Hampton
Nearest Bus Station: Hounslow/Kingston
Club Shop: At the ground
Opening Times: Matchdays only
Telephone Nº: –
Police Telephone Nº: (020) 8577-1212

GROUND INFORMATION
Away Supporters' Entrances & Sections:
No usual segregation

ADMISSION INFO (2007/2008 PRICES)
Adult Standing: £8.00
Adult Seating: £8.00
Senior Citizen/Concessionary Standing: £5.00
Senior Citizen/Concessionary Seating: £5.00
Junior Standing: £5.00 (Ages 4-16)
Junior Seating: £5.00 (Ages 4-16)
Programme Price: £1.50

DISABLED INFORMATION
Wheelchairs: Accommodated
Helpers: Admitted
Prices: Normal prices apply
Disabled Toilets: None
Contact: (020) 8979-2456   (Bookings are necessary)

Travelling Supporters' Information:
Routes: From the South: Exit the M3 at Junction 1 and follow the A308 (signposted Kingston). Turn 1st left after Kempton Park into Percy Road. Turn right at the level crossing into Station Road then left into Beaver Close for the ground; From the North: Take the A305 from Twickenham then turn left onto the A311. Pass through Hampton Hill onto Hampton High Street. Turn right at the White Hart pub (just before the junction with the A308), then right into Station Road and right again into Beaver Close.

HAVANT & WATERLOOVILLE FC

Founded: 1998
Former Names: Formed by the amalgamation of Waterlooville FC and Havant Town FC
Nickname: 'The Hawks'
Ground: West Leigh Park, Martin Road, Havant, PO9 5TH
Record Attendance: 5,757 (2006/07)
Pitch Size: 112 × 76 yards

Colours: White shirts and shorts
Telephone N°: (023) 9278-7822 (Ground)
Fax Number: (023) 9226-2367
Ground Capacity: 5,800
Seating Capacity: 562
Correspondence: Trevor Brock, 2 Betula Close, Waterlooville, PO7 8EJ **Phone**: (023) 9226-7276
Web site: www.havantandwaterlooville.net

GENERAL INFORMATION

Supporters Club: None, but large Social Club
Telephone N°: (023) 9278-7855
Car Parking: Space for 750 cars at the ground
Coach Parking: At the ground
Nearest Railway Station: Havant (1 mile)
Nearest Bus Station: Town Centre (1½ miles)
Club Shop: At the ground
Opening Times: Daily
Telephone N°: (023) 9278-7822
Police Telephone N°: (0845) 454545

GROUND INFORMATION

Away Supporters' Entrances & Sections:
Martin Road End

ADMISSION INFO (2007/2008 PRICES)

Adult Standing: £8.00
Adult Seating: £10.00
Senior Citizen Standing/Seating: £6.00
Note: When accompanied by a paying adult, children under the age of 11 are admitted free of charge
Programme Price: £2.00

DISABLED INFORMATION

Wheelchairs: 12 spaces available in the Main Stand
Helpers: Admitted
Prices: Normal prices for disabled fans. Free for helpers
Disabled Toilets: Two available
Contact: (023) 9226-7276   (Bookings are necessary)

Travelling Supporters' Information:
Routes: From London or the North take the A27 from Chichester and exit at the B2149 turn-off for Havant. Take the 2nd exit off the dual carriageway into Bartons Road and then the 1st right into Martin Road for the ground; From the West: Take the M27 then the A27 to the Petersfield exit. Then as above.

HAYES & YEADING FC

Founded: 2007
Former Names: Formed by the amalgamation of Hayes FC and Yeading FC in 2007
Nickname: –
Ground: Church Road, Hayes, Middlesex UB3 2LE
Record Attendance: 15,370 (10/2/1951)
Pitch Size: 117 × 70 yards

Colours: Red shirts with Black shorts
Telephone Nº: (020) 8573-2075
Fax Number: (020) 8573-0933
Ground Capacity: 4,300
Seating Capacity: 500
Web site: www.hyufc.net

GENERAL INFORMATION

Supporters Club: Lee Hermitage, c/o Hayes FC
Telephone Nº: (020) 8573-2075
Car Parking: 300 spaces available at the ground
Coach Parking: By arrangement
Nearest Railway Station: Hayes & Harlington (1 mile)
Nearest Bus Station: Hayes
Club Shop: At the ground
Opening Times: Matchdays only. Saturday matches from 2.00pm–5.00pm. Weekday matches from 6.45pm–9.30pm
Telephone Nº: (020) 8573-2075
Police Telephone Nº: (020) 8900-7212

GROUND INFORMATION

Away Supporters' Entrances & Sections:
Church Road End when segregated (not usual)

ADMISSION INFO (2007/2008 PRICES)

Adult Standing: £9.00
Adult Seating: £10.00
Child/Senior Citizen Standing: £5.00
Child/Senior Citizen Seating: £6.00
Programme Price: £2.00

DISABLED INFORMATION

Wheelchairs: Accommodated as necessary
Helpers: Admitted
Prices: £10.00 for the disabled but a helper is admitted free of charge with each paying disabled fan
Disabled Toilets: Available
Contact: (020) 8573-2075   (Bookings are not necessary)

Travelling Supporters' Information:
Routes: From the A40: Approaching London, take the Ruislip junction – turn right onto the B455 Ruislip Road to the White Hart Roundabout. Take the Hayes bypass to Uxbridge Road (A4020), turn right, then Church Road is ¾ mile on the left, opposite the Adam & Eve pub; From the M4: Exit at Junction 3 and take the A312 to Parkway towards Southall, then the Hayes bypass to Uxbridge Road (A4020). Turn left, then as above.

LEWES FC

Founded: 1885
Former Names: None
Nickname: 'Rooks'
Ground: The Dripping Pan, Mountfield Road,
Lewes   BN7 1XN
Record Attendance: 2,500 (vs Newhaven 26/12/47)
Pitch Size: 109 × 74 yards

Colours: Red & Black striped shirts with Black shorts
Telephone Nº: (01273) 472100
Fax Number: (01273) 474788
Ground Capacity: 3,000
Seating Capacity: 500
Web site: www.lewesfc.com

GENERAL INFORMATION
Supporters Club: c/o Club
Telephone Nº: (01273) 472100
Car Parking: At the ground
Coach Parking: At Lewes Railway Station (adjacent)
Nearest Railway Station: Lewes (adjacent)
Nearest Bus Station: Lewes (½ mile)
Club Shop: At the ground.
Opening Times: Matchdays only

GROUND INFORMATION
Away Supporters' Entrances & Sections:
No segregation

ADMISSION INFO (2007/2008 PRICES)
Adult Standing: £10.00
Adult Seating: £10.00
Junior Standing: £2.00 (Under-14s)
Junior Seating: £2.00 (Under-14s)
Senior Citizen/Under-16s Standing: £5.00
Senior Citizen/Under-16s Seating: £5.00
Programme Price: £2.00

DISABLED INFORMATION
Wheelchairs: Accommodated
Helpers: Admitted
Prices: Normal prices apply for the disabled and helpers
Disabled Toilets: Available
Contact: (01273) 472100

Travelling Supporters' Information:
Routes: From the North: Take the A26 or the A275 to Lewes and follow signs for the Railway Station. Pass the station on the left and take the next left. The ground is adjacent; From the South and West: Take the A27 to the A26 for the Town Centre. Then as above.

MAIDENHEAD UNITED FC

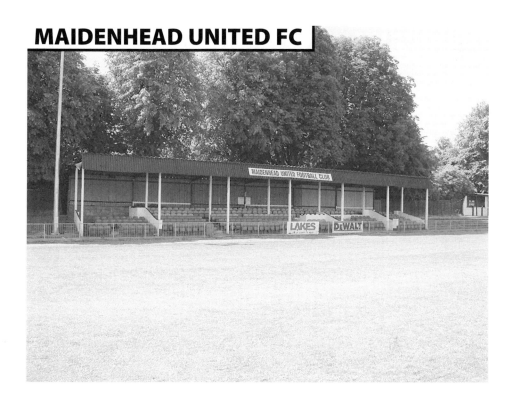

Founded: 1870
Former Names: None
Nickname: 'Magpies'
Ground: York Road, Maidenhead, Berks. SL6 1SF
Record Attendance: 7,920 (1936)
Pitch Size: 110 × 75 yards

Colours: Black and White striped shirts, White shorts
Telephone Nº: (01628) 636314 (Club)
Contact Number: (01628) 636078
Ground Capacity: 4,500
Seating Capacity: 400
Web site: www.maidenheadunitedfc.co.uk

GENERAL INFORMATION
Supporters Club: c/o Club
Telephone Nº: (01628) 636314
Car Parking: Street parking
Coach Parking: Street parking
Nearest Railway Station: Maidenhead (¼ mile)
Nearest Bus Station: Maidenhead
Club Shop: At the ground
Opening Times: Matchdays only
Telephone Nº: (01628) 624739
Police Telephone Nº: –

GROUND INFORMATION
Away Supporters' Entrances & Sections:
No usual segregation

ADMISSION INFO (2007/2008 PRICES)
Adult Standing: £9.00
Adult Seating: £9.00
Concessionary Standing and Seating: £5.00
Child Standing and Seating: £2.00 (Under-16s)
Programme Price: £2.00

DISABLED INFORMATION
Wheelchairs: Accommodated
Helpers: Admitted
Prices: Normal prices for the disabled. Free for helpers
Disabled Toilets: Available
Contact: (01628) 636078   (Bookings are not necessary)

Travelling Supporters' Information:
Routes: Exit M4 at Junction 7 and take the A4 to Maidenhead. Cross the River Thames bridge and turn left at the 2nd roundabout passing through the traffic lights. York Road is first right and the ground is approximately 300 yards along on the left.

NEWPORT COUNTY FC

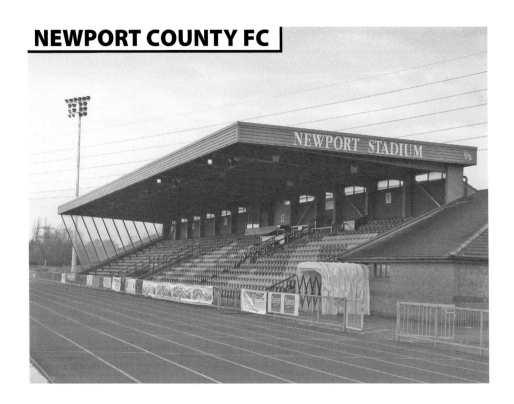

Founded: 1989
Former Names: Newport AFC
Nickname: 'The Exiles'
Ground: Newport Stadium, Stadium Way, Newport
International Sports Village, Newport NP19 4PT
Record Attendance: 4,616 (11th November 2006)
Pitch Size: 112 × 72 yards

Colours: Amber shirts with Black shorts
Telephone Nº: (01633) 662262
Fax Number: (01633) 666107
Ground Capacity: 4,300
Seating Capacity: 1,236
Web site: www.newport-county.co.uk

GENERAL INFORMATION
Supporters Club: Bob Herrin, c/o Club
Telephone Nº: (01633) 274440
Car Parking: Space for 500 cars at the ground
Coach Parking: At the ground
Nearest Railway Station: Newport
Nearest Bus Station: Newport
Club Shop: At the ground
Opening Times: Matchdays only
Telephone Nº: (01633) 662262
Police Telephone Nº: (01633) 244999

GROUND INFORMATION
Away Supporters' Entrances & Sections:
No segregation unless specifically required by Police

ADMISSION INFO (2007/2008 PRICES)
Adult Standing: £9.00
Adult Seating: £9.00
Senior Citizen Standing: £6.00
Senior Citizen Seating: £6.00
Juniors: £2.00
Programme Price: £2.00

DISABLED INFORMATION
Wheelchairs: Accommodated
Helpers: Admitted
Prices: Normal prices for the disabled. Free for helpers
Disabled Toilets: Yes
Contact: (01633) 662262   (Bookings are not necessary)

Travelling Supporters' Information:
Routes: Exit the M4 at Junction 24 and take the A48 exit at the roundabout, signposted 'Newport Int. Sports Village'. Go straight on at the first two roundabouts then bear left at the 3rd roundabout. Carry straight on over the next two roundabouts, then turn left between the two Carcraft buildings. Take the 1st turning on the left into the Stadium car park.

ST. ALBANS CITY FC

Founded: 1908
Former Names: None
Nickname: 'The Saints'
Ground: Clarence Park, York Road, St. Albans, Hertfordshire AL1 4PL
Record Attendance: 9,757 (27/2/26)
Pitch Size: 110 × 80 yards

Colours: Yellow shirts with Blue trim, Yellow shorts
Telephone Nº: (01727) 864296
Fax Number: (01727) 866235
Ground Capacity: 5,007
Seating Capacity: 667
Web site: www.sacfc.co.uk

GENERAL INFORMATION

Supporters Club: Ian Rogers, c/o Club
Telephone Nº: –
Car Parking: Street parking
Coach Parking: In Clarence Park
Nearest Railway Station: St. Albans City (200 yds)
Nearest Bus Station: City Centre (short walk)
Club Shop: At the ground
Opening Times: Matchdays only
Telephone Nº: (01727) 864296
Police Telephone Nº: (01727) 276122

GROUND INFORMATION

Away Supporters' Entrances & Sections:
Hatfield Road End when matches are segregated

ADMISSION INFO (2007/2008 PRICES)

Adult Standing: £10.00
Adult Seating: £12.00
Under-12s Standing: £3.00   **OAP/Under-16s**: £5.00
Under-12s Seating: £3.00   **OAP/Under-16s**: £6.00
Programme Price: £2.00

DISABLED INFORMATION

Wheelchairs: Accommodated
Helpers: One admitted per disabled supporter
Prices: Free for the disabled, concessionary prices for the helpers
Disabled Toilets: Available inside new Building at the York Road End
Contact: (01727) 864296 (Bookings are not necessary)

Travelling Supporters' Information:
Routes: Take the M1 or M10 to the A405 North Orbital Road and at the roundabout at the start of the M10, go north on the A5183 (Watling Street). Turn right along St. Stephen's Hill and carry along into St. Albans. Continue up Holywell Hill, go through two sets of traffic lights and at the end of St. Peter's Street, take a right turn at the roundabout into Hatfield Road. Follow over the mini-roundabouts and at the second set of traffic lights turn left into Clarence Road and the ground is on the left. Park in Clarence Road and enter the ground via the Park or in York Road and use the entrance by the footbridge.

SUTTON UNITED FC

Founded: 1898
Former Names: Formed by the amalgamation of Sutton Guild Rovers FC and Sutton Association FC
Nickname: 'U's'
Ground: Borough Sports Ground, Gander Green Lane, Sutton, Surrey   SM1 2EY
Record Attendance: 14,000 (1970)
Pitch Size: 110 × 72 yards

Colours: Chocolate and Amber shirts with Chocolate-coloured shorts
Telephone Nº: (020) 8644-4440
Fax Number: (020) 8644-5120
Ground Capacity: 7,032
Seating Capacity: 765
Web site: www.suttonunited.net

GENERAL INFORMATION

Supporters Club: Alison Denyer, c/o Club
Telephone Nº: –
Car Parking: 150 spaces behind the Main Stand
Coach Parking: Space for 1 coach in the car park
Nearest Railway Station: West Sutton (adjacent)
Nearest Bus Station: Sutton
Club Shop: At the ground
Opening Times: Matchdays only
Telephone Nº: (020) 8644-4440
Police Telephone Nº: (020) 8680-1212

GROUND INFORMATION

Away Supporters' Entrances & Sections:
Collingwood Road entrances and accommodation

ADMISSION INFO (2007/2008 PRICES)

Adult Standing: £10.00
Adult Seating: £11.00
Child Standing: £3.00
Child Seating: £4.00
Senior Citizen Standing: £5.00
Senior Citizen Seating: £6.00
Programme Price: £2.00

DISABLED INFORMATION

Wheelchairs: 8 spaces are available under cover accommodated on the track perimeter
Helpers: Admitted
Prices: Normal prices apply
Disabled Toilets: Available alongside the Standing Terrace
Contact: (020) 8644-4440   (Bookings are necessary)

Travelling Supporters' Information:
Routes: Exit the M25 at Junction 8 (Reigate Hill) and travel North on the A217 for approximately 8 miles. Cross the A232 then turn right at the traffic lights (past Goose & Granit Public House) into Gander Green Lane. The ground is 300 yards on the left; From London: Gander Green Lane crosses the Sutton bypass 1 mile south of Rose Hill Roundabout. Avoid Sutton Town Centre, especially on Saturdays.

THURROCK FC

Founded: 1985
Former Names: Purfleet FC
Nickname: 'Fleet'
Ground: Thurrock Hotel, Ship Lane, Grays, Essex, RM19 1YN   **Telephone Nº**: (01708) 865492
Record Attendance: 2,572 (1998)
Pitch Size: 113 × 72 yards

Colours: Yellow and Green shirts with Green shorts
Tel Nº: (01708) 868901 (Hotel) or 865492 (Clubhouse)
Contact Nº: (01708) 458301 (Secretary)
Fax Number: (01708) 868863
Ground Capacity: 4,200
Seating Capacity: 500
Web site: www.thurrockfc.com

GENERAL INFORMATION

Supporters Club: None
Car Parking: At the ground
Coach Parking: At the ground
Nearest Railway Station: Purfleet (2 miles)
Nearest Bus Station: Grays Town Centre
Club Shop: At the ground
Opening Times: Matchdays only
Telephone Nº: (01708) 865492
Police Telephone Nº: (01375) 391212

GROUND INFORMATION

Away Supporters' Entrances & Sections:
No usual segregation

ADMISSION INFO (2007/2008 PRICES)

Adult Standing: £10.00
Adult Seating: £10.00
Child Standing: £2.00
Child Seating: £2.00
Senior Citizen Standing: £6.00
Senior Citizen Seating: £6.00
Programme Price: £2.00

DISABLED INFORMATION

Wheelchairs: No special area but accommodated
Helpers: Admitted
Prices: Free for the disabled. Helpers pay normal prices
Disabled Toilets: Available in the Clubhouse
Contact: (01708) 865492   (Bookings are not necessary)

Travelling Supporters' Information:
Routes: Take the M25 or A13 to the Dartford Tunnel roundabout. The ground is then 50 yards on the right along Ship Lane.

WELLING UNITED FC

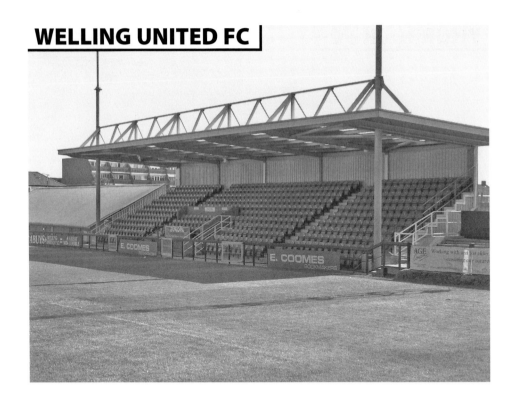

Founded: 1963
Former Names: None
Nickname: 'The Wings'
Ground: Park View Road Ground, Welling, Kent, DA16 1SY
Record Attendance: 4,020 (1989/90)
Pitch Size: 112 × 72 yards

Colours: Shirts are Red with White facings, Red shorts
Telephone Nº: (0208) 301-1196
Daytime Phone Nº: (0208) 301-1196
Fax Number: (0208) 301-5676
Ground Capacity: 4,000
Seating Capacity: 500
Web site: www.wellingunited.com

GENERAL INFORMATION

Supporters Club: –
Car Parking: Street parking only
Coach Parking: Outside of the ground
Nearest Railway Station: Welling (¾ mile)
Nearest Bus Station: Bexleyheath
Club Shop: At the ground
Opening Times: Matchdays only
Telephone Nº: (0208) 301-1196
Police Telephone Nº: (0208) 304-3161

GROUND INFORMATION

Away Supporters' Entrances & Sections:
Accommodation in the Danson Park End

ADMISSION INFO (2007/2008 PRICES)

Adult Standing: £10.00
Adult Seating: £11.00
Senior Citizen/Child Standing: £6.00
Senior Citizen/Child Seating: £7.00
Under-12s: £3.00
Programme Price: £2.00

DISABLED INFORMATION

Wheelchairs: Accommodated at the side of the Main Stand
Helpers: Admitted
Prices: £6.00 for the disabled. Helpers pay normal prices
Disabled Toilets: Yes
Contact: (0208) 301-1196   (Bookings are not necessary)

Travelling Supporters' Information:
Routes: Take the A2 (Rochester Way) from London, then the A221 Northwards (Danson Road) to Bexleyheath. At the end turn left towards Welling along Park View Road and the ground is on the left.

WESTON-SUPER-MARE FC

Founded: 1899
Former Names: Christ Church Old Boys FC
Nickname: 'Seagulls'
Ground: Woodspring Stadium, Winterstoke Road, Weston-Super-Mare   BS24 9AA
Record Attendance: 2,623   (vs Woking in F.A. Cup)
Pitch Size: 110 × 70 yards

Colours: White shirts with Blue shorts
Telephone N°: (01934) 621618
Fax Number: (01934) 622704
Ground Capacity: 3,071
Seating Capacity: 278
Web site: www.westonsupermareafc.co.uk

GENERAL INFORMATION

Supporters Club: Joe Varian, 336 Milton Road, Weston-Super-Mare
Telephone N°: (01934) 627929
Car Parking: 140 spaces available at the ground
Coach Parking: At the ground
Nearest Railway Station: Weston-Super-Mare (1½ miles)
Nearest Bus Station: Weston-Super-Mare (1½ miles)
Club Shop: At the ground
Opening Times: Matchdays only
Telephone N°: (01934) 621618
Police Telephone N°: (01275) 818181

GROUND INFORMATION

Away Supporters' Entrances & Sections:
No usual segregation

ADMISSION INFO (2007/2008 PRICES)

Adult Standing/Seating: £8.50
Senior Citizen/Student Standing/Seating: £5.50
Child Standing/Seating: Free of charge (Under-16s)
Programme Price: £1.50

DISABLED INFORMATION

Wheelchairs: Accommodated in a special disabled section
Helpers: Admitted
Prices: Normal prices apply
Disabled Toilets: One available
Contact: (01934) 621618   (Bookings are not necessary)

Travelling Supporters' Information:
Routes: Exit the M5 at Junction 21 and follow the dual carriageway (A370) to the 4th roundabout (Asda Winterstoke). Turn left, go over the mini-roundabout and continue for 800 yards. The ground is on the right.

Football Conference National — 2006/2007 Season

	Aldershot Town	Altrincham	Burton Albion	Cambridge United	Crawley Town	Dagenham & Redbridge	Exeter City	Forest Green Rovers	Gravesend & Northfleet	Grays Athletic	Halifax Town	Kidderminster Harriers	Morecambe	Northwich Victoria	Oxford United	Rushden & Diamonds	Southport	St. Alban's City	Stafford Rangers	Stevenage Borough	Tamworth	Weymouth	Woking	York City
Aldershot Town	■	0-0	3-2	0-1	0-2	1-1	3-2	2-1	3-2	1-0	1-0	4-2	0-1	1-3	1-1	2-2	2-2	2-0	4-2	4-0	3-3	1-0	2-2	0-2
Altrincham	0-0	■	2-3	5-0	1-1	0-5	1-2	2-2	0-2	1-0	1-0	0-1	0-2	3-0	0-3	2-1	2-1	2-0	0-1	2-1	2-0	0-0	2-3	0-4
Burton Albion	1-3	2-1	■	2-1	2-1	0-2	1-0	1-0	0-1	3-0	1-0	1-1	2-1	2-0	1-2	1-2	0-1	1-0	0-0	2-1	1-0	1-1	2-1	1-2
Cambridge United	2-0	2-2	1-2	■	1-2	4-2	1-3	1-1	3-0	2-0	1-2	1-1	1-3	0-1	0-3	0-1	2-2	0-2	0-1	1-0	1-0	7-0	3-0	0-5
Crawley Town	1-2	1-1	1-0	1-1	■	0-0	0-3	3-1	1-1	0-1	2-0	0-0	4-0	0-2	0-1	1-0	2-1	2-1	1-2	3-0	1-0	0-3	0-0	3-0
Dagenham & Redbridge	2-1	4-1	3-0	2-0	2-1	■	4-1	1-1	2-1	0-0	1-0	1-3	2-1	5-0	0-1	1-2	0-0	4-2	1-1	2-0	4-0	4-1	3-2	2-1
Exeter City	0-0	2-1	3-0	0-1	1-1	3-2	■	1-0	1-3	2-1	4-1	1-1	1-0	1-1	2-1	0-0	2-1	4-2	1-1	1-1	4-0	1-0	1-1	1-1
Forest Green Rovers	3-0	2-2	1-0	1-1	1-0	0-1	2-1	■	0-1	0-0	2-0	2-1	1-3	2-1	1-5	0-2	1-2	2-2	2-1	4-4	2-0	3-2	2-3	0-1
Gravesend & Northfleet	1-1	3-1	0-0	2-0	1-0	0-0	2-2	1-1	■	2-0	2-0	1-3	2-1	3-0	1-0	1-0	0-4	3-2	1-4	1-1	4-1	1-3	1-0	0-1
Grays Athletic	1-2	1-1	0-1	1-1	0-0	0-1	2-2	1-1	0-2	■	1-0	3-0	0-1	1-0	2-2	3-1	4-0	2-1	1-1	0-2	1-0	2-2	3-0	0-0
Halifax Town	2-0	1-1	1-2	1-0	2-1	3-1	2-1	2-2	1-1	0-2	■	2-0	1-1	0-2	1-1	0-0	1-1	3-1	2-1	3-1	1-4	3-0	1-1	1-1
Kidderminster Harriers	0-0	3-2	0-0	1-0	0-1	1-4	0-2	2-2	1-2	2-1	1-0	■	0-1	0-1	0-0	0-0	2-0	1-3	2-0	1-2	0-2	0-1	0-1	2-1
Morecambe	2-1	0-1	0-1	2-2	1-0	1-1	2-2	1-1	1-0	1-0	4-0	0-1	■	2-1	0-3	1-0	2-0	1-0	3-3	0-0	2-0	2-0	2-0	1-3
Northwich Victoria	1-3	1-1	0-3	0-4	2-1	2-0	1-0	2-0	1-2	0-3	3-2	1-0	0-2	■	1-0	4-1	3-1	0-3	4-0	0-0	1-0	0-1	0-2	1-2
Oxford United	2-0	1-1	0-0	1-1	1-1	2-2	1-0	0-2	1-0	1-1	2-0	1-0	0-0	5-1	■	0-1	2-2	2-1	2-0	2-0	2-1	4-1	0-0	2-0
Rushden & Diamonds	0-1	3-0	1-2	3-1	1-1	2-3	3-0	2-0	0-0	1-3	0-1	0-1	2-2	1-0	1-0	■	2-3	1-0	2-1	2-2	1-1	4-1	2-0	0-1
Southport	1-0	2-1	3-1	1-2	3-1	1-4	0-1	1-2	2-3	3-1	1-1	1-1	1-2	1-2	0-1	1-2	■	1-1	5-1	1-2	1-0	0-1	0-1	0-1
St. Alban's City	3-5	1-5	0-1	0-0	2-2	1-2	1-2	0-2	2-3	0-6	3-2	1-0	1-2	0-3	0-2	3-2	2-2	■	0-3	2-3	1-0	1-0	0-1	4-2
Stafford Rangers	0-3	1-0	1-1	1-2	0-1	1-2	0-1	0-1	3-1	4-2	2-3	1-2	1-3	2-0	0-1	1-1	1-0	2-2	■	1-3	0-4	2-0	1-0	0-0
Stevenage Borough	3-2	0-1	2-1	4-1	2-3	1-2	0-0	3-3	3-0	1-0	2-1	3-3	0-2	2-2	1-0	3-1	1-2	6-0	3-0	■	3-0	1-0	3-2	1-2
Tamworth	2-0	1-0	0-1	0-1	0-2	1-0	1-1	2-1	4-2	1-0	0-0	0-1	0-1	1-3	1-4	1-1	1-1	0-0	2-1	1-3	■	1-3	3-1	2-2
Weymouth	1-0	1-2	1-1	2-1	3-2	1-1	2-1	1-0	2-1	1-3	1-0	1-1	2-1	1-1	1-1	2-0	2-1	1-2	0-1	3-1	2-1	■	2-3	1-2
Woking	2-0	2-0	0-0	0-1	1-2	2-2	0-2	3-3	2-2	1-0	2-2	3-0	1-1	3-2	1-0	3-0	1-1	1-2	1-1	0-1	1-1	0-2	■	1-2
York City	1-0	1-0	3-2	1-2	5-0	2-3	0-0	0-0	0-2	2-2	2-0	0-1	2-3	2-1	1-0	3-1	2-2	0-0	5-0	0-1	0-1	0-2	1-0	■

Nationwide Conference National

Season 2006/2007

Team	P	W	D	L	F	A	Pts
Dagenham & Redbridge	46	28	11	7	93	48	95
Oxford United	46	22	15	9	66	33	81
Morecambe	46	23	12	11	64	46	81
York City	46	23	11	12	65	45	80
Exeter City	46	22	12	12	67	48	78
Burton Albion	46	22	9	15	52	47	75
Gravesend & Northfleet	46	21	11	14	63	56	74
Stevenage Borough	46	20	10	16	76	66	70
Aldershot Town	46	18	11	17	64	62	65
Kidderminster Harriers	46	17	12	17	43	50	63
Weymouth	46	18	9	19	56	73	63
Rushden & Diamonds	46	17	11	18	58	54	62
Northwich Victoria	46	18	4	24	51	69	58
Forest Green Rovers	46	13	18	15	59	64	57
Woking	46	15	12	19	56	61	57
Halifax Town	46	15	10	21	55	62	55
Cambridge United	46	15	10	21	57	66	55
Crawley Town	46	17	12	17	52	52	53
Grays Athletic	46	13	13	20	56	55	52
Stafford Rangers	46	14	10	22	49	71	52
Altrincham	46	13	12	21	53	67	51
Tamworth	46	13	9	24	43	61	48
Southport	46	11	14	21	57	67	47
St. Alban's City	46	10	10	26	57	89	40

Crawley Town had 10 points deducted.

Promotion Play-offs

Exeter City 0   Oxford United 1
York City 0   Morecambe 0

Oxford United 1   Exeter City .... 2 (aet)
Exeter City won 4-3 on penalties
Morecambe 2   York City .... 1 (aet)
Morecambe won 2-1 on aggregate

Exeter City 1   Morecambe 2

Promoted: Dagenham & Redbridge and Morecambe
Relegated: Altrincham, Tamworth, Southport and St. Albans City

Football Conference North 2006/2007 Season	Alfreton Town	Barrow	Blyth Spartans	Droylsden	Farsley Celtic	Gainsborough Trinity	Harrogate Town	Hinckley United	Hucknall Town	Hyde United	Kettering Town	Lancaster City	Leigh RMI	Moor Green	Nuneaton Borough	Redditch United	Scarborough	Stalybridge Celtic	Vauxhall Motors	Worcester City	Workington	Worksop Town
Alfreton Town		1-0	0-1	1-3	0-1	3-1	0-0	0-1	2-1	2-2	1-1	2-1	1-0	3-0	0-3	0-0	1-1	1-2	2-0	0-2	1-1	3-0
Barrow	1-1		0-2	2-1	2-2	3-0	2-3	1-0	1-0	1-2	0-1	3-0	2-0	1-1	0-1	0-4	1-1	2-1	0-0	0-1	0-0	1-2
Blyth Spartans	3-0	1-0		0-3	4-1	2-0	0-0	3-1	2-2	0-0	2-2	3-0	1-0	0-1	1-2	1-2	2-0	1-0	1-2	2-2	0-2	2-0
Droylsden	1-1	2-1	0-0		4-1	2-1	2-0	3-1	5-3	4-2	1-1	6-1	2-2	1-0	4-2	2-1	1-3	6-1	1-0	2-1	2-1	3-2
Farsley Celtic	1-1	2-2	3-0	0-3		1-0	1-0	0-2	1-0	1-1	2-1	3-1	1-1	0-1	0-1	4-0	0-2	1-1	3-2	1-0	1-2	1-0
Gainsborough Trinity	4-0	1-0	0-2	3-2	0-0		1-3	1-0	2-3	2-3	2-3	1-0	0-0	1-0	1-1	2-2	3-1	2-0	1-2	1-3	1-0	1-1
Harrogate Town	0-1	1-1	1-2	1-1	1-0	1-1		2-0	1-1	1-2	2-3	3-0	2-1	1-1	1-1	2-2	0-1	0-0	1-1	1-0	4-0	1-0
Hinckley United	2-2	1-1	2-1	2-1	2-1	1-1	0-1		1-1	2-0	3-1	5-0	3-1	2-0	2-2	3-1	1-1	2-3	1-1	3-3	2-1	0-1
Hucknall Town	0-2	1-3	1-2	2-2	0-1	3-3	0-3	1-2		4-2	1-2	5-0	1-3	3-2	2-1	2-2	0-1	2-1	2-2	4-2	2-1	4-0
Hyde United	2-1	1-1	5-1	2-1	3-4	3-0	4-0	2-0	1-0		3-5	5-0	2-0	4-1	3-2	0-2	1-1	3-1	1-1	0-0	1-1	1-2
Kettering Town	0-1	3-2	1-1	1-0	3-2	4-2	3-1	1-2	0-0	1-0		3-3	4-0	1-1	3-2	3-1	3-1	2-1	0-1	1-1	2-3	2-2
Lancaster City	0-2	0-2	0-2	1-2	1-2	0-1	0-2	1-4	0-1	2-3	0-1		0-0	0-3	0-4	1-2	1-5	0-1	2-2	0-2	1-5	0-3
Leigh RMI	2-0	0-3	3-1	2-2	1-3	2-0	1-3	2-3	4-3	2-0	1-2	0-1		2-2	1-0	0-0	1-1	1-3	0-3	2-1	2-0	2-1
Moor Green	2-0	0-0	0-2	5-2	1-1	2-1	0-1	0-1	1-2	1-1	1-2	3-1	0-0		1-1	1-1	1-2	2-1	5-2	3-1	1-0	0-1
Nuneaton Borough	1-0	3-0	1-1	1-0	1-1	0-1	0-0	0-1	2-1	0-0	2-1	1-0	0-1	0-1		1-0	1-1	3-2	1-1	1-1	0-0	0-0
Redditch United	3-2	1-1	0-2	0-0	1-4	1-1	2-1	1-3	1-2	2-1	4-4	2-2	2-1	0-1	2-0		1-1	1-2	3-3	1-2	4-1	0-1
Scarborough	0-1	1-1	0-1	1-0	0-0	0-0	1-1	3-0	1-2	1-2	1-1	1-2	1-1	3-0	1-3	3-2		0-1	0-1	1-0	0-1	2-1
Stalybridge Celtic	3-2	0-4	3-2	1-2	0-2	0-2	0-2	2-2	2-2	3-7	0-0	3-1	2-1	2-3	4-3	3-2	2-2		3-3	1-1	1-2	3-0
Vauxhall Motors	1-2	0-1	2-0	2-3	1-2	0-1	1-5	2-2	1-2	1-0	1-1	4-1	2-1	1-1	1-3	1-1	1-1	2-2		2-0	1-2	2-0
Worcester City	0-0	3-0	3-2	3-1	0-1	1-1	2-3	3-1	2-0	2-2	2-0	4-1	1-2	0-1	3-3	1-1	3-2	1-1	3-3		2-2	2-1
Workington	1-1	1-1	3-0	0-0	3-0	1-2	3-2	1-1	1-0	3-1	2-0	1-1	0-1	3-2	2-0	1-0	0-1	2-1	2-0	0-1		3-2
Worksop Town	2-0	2-0	1-1	0-2	2-2	1-2	0-0	1-1	1-3	3-1	0-2	3-1	2-0	0-1	0-0	2-3	0-0	2-1	1-4	0-2	1-3	

Nationwide Conference North

Season 2006/2007

Droylsden	42	23	9	10	85	55	78
Kettering Town	42	20	13	9	75	58	73
Workington	42	20	10	12	61	46	70
Hinckley United	42	19	12	11	68	54	69
Farsley Celtic	42	19	11	12	58	51	68
Harrogate Town	42	18	13	11	58	41	67
Blyth Spartans	42	19	9	14	57	49	66
Hyde United	42	18	11	13	79	62	65
Worcester City	42	16	14	12	67	54	62
Nuneaton Borough	42	15	15	12	54	45	60
Moor Green	42	16	11	15	53	51	59
Gainsborough Trinity	42	15	11	16	51	57	56
Hucknall Town	42	15	9	18	69	69	54
Alfreton Town	42	14	12	16	44	50	54
Vauxhall Motors	42	12	15	15	62	64	51
Barrow	42	12	14	16	47	48	50
Leigh RMI	42	13	10	19	47	61	49
Stalybridge Celtic	42	13	10	19	64	81	49
Redditch United	42	11	15	16	61	68	48
Scarborough	42	13	16	13	50	45	45
Worksop Town	42	12	9	21	44	62	45
Lancaster City	42	2	5	35	27	110	1

Scarborough and Lancaster City each had 10 points deducted.

Promotion Play-offs North

Farsley Celtic .... 1 Kettering Town 1
Hinckley United .... 0 Workington 0

Kettering Town .... 0 Farsley Celtic .... 0 (aet)
Farsley Celtic won 4-2 on penalties
Workington .... 1 Hinckley United 2
Hinckley United won 2-1 on aggregate

Farsley Celtic .... 4 Hinckley United 3

Promoted from Conference North: Droylsden and Farsley Celtic

Football Conference South 2006/2007 Season	Basingstoke Town	Bedford Town	Bishop's Stortford	Bognor Regis Town	Braintree Town	Cambridge City	Dorchester Town	Eastbourne Borough	Eastleigh	Farnborough Town	Fisher Athletic	Havant & Waterlooville	Hayes	Histon	Lewes	Newport County	Salisbury City	Sutton United	Thurrock	Welling United	Weston-super-Mare	Yeading
Basingstoke Town		0-1	1-0	4-0	1-2	0-0	2-2	0-1	0-1	0-2	2-1	2-1	1-1	1-2	0-0	0-1	1-1	0-2	1-1	1-3	0-1	1-3
Bedford Town	0-0		3-1	2-3	1-2	0-1	1-1	1-1	1-1	0-2	1-4	2-1	1-2	0-2	0-2	0-2	1-2	2-0	3-1	2-2	2-1	2-5
Bishop's Stortford	3-1	2-2		0-1	0-2	2-1	4-3	1-0	1-1	2-1	2-2	1-0	3-1	0-0	3-0	2-2	1-1	3-2	2-1	1-3	2-2	2-0
Bognor Regis Town	1-2	1-0	2-4		1-2	0-1	3-0	1-1	0-0	1-1	1-1	0-0	5-1	0-0	1-1	1-1	1-1	0-4	3-0	1-1	3-1	3-1
Braintree Town	1-0	2-0	3-1	1-2		2-1	3-1	1-1	1-1	2-1	2-2	0-0	0-1	1-1	1-1	2-1	0-0	0-1	0-1	2-1	0-1	3-1
Cambridge City	0-1	0-0	0-1	2-0	1-0		0-1	1-0	2-0	1-1	0-0	3-0	2-2	0-1	1-0	2-1	1-3	2-3	2-3	0-1	2-3	3-0
Dorchester Town	1-2	1-3	0-1	0-1	0-0	3-1		0-0	1-0	4-1	1-3	1-3	0-2	1-2	1-5	0-4	0-3	5-4	3-1	0-1	1-5	3-2
Eastbourne Borough	1-1	0-3	2-1	2-0	1-2	2-1	1-1		0-0	0-0	3-1	1-1	0-0	1-1	2-1	2-1	1-0	2-0	3-1	0-0	3-0	2-0
Eastleigh	3-1	2-0	1-1	0-4	0-3	0-1	1-1	1-1		3-1	4-0	0-1	2-1	1-0	0-0	3-1	0-1	1-0	1-1	1-3	1-1	1-4
Farnborough Town	1-1	3-2	3-1	3-1	2-1	2-1	1-1	1-0	1-0		2-0	2-1	1-3	2-3	1-1	1-0	0-1	4-0	2-1	2-1	0-0	2-1
Fisher Athletic	3-3	3-0	0-1	3-0	3-0	3-0	1-1	0-3	3-1	3-0		3-3	3-0	1-4	5-1	3-3	1-4	2-1	3-5	2-1	1-1	3-1
Havant & Waterlooville	1-0	4-0	5-4	2-2	1-1	2-3	2-0	2-1	1-1	2-0	1-3		6-0	2-1	1-1	3-1	3-1	1-0	3-0	4-0	2-1	4-0
Hayes	1-1	3-1	1-2	2-3	2-3	0-1	4-0	1-1	2-1	1-1	4-3	0-1		1-3	1-4	0-1	0-4	0-4	1-1	0-1	1-0	0-1
Histon	4-2	1-0	0-2	2-1	2-0	2-1	3-0	1-2	1-0	2-1	2-1	4-0	5-0		3-2	1-0	4-2	2-1	3-1	1-0	3-2	1-2
Lewes	2-2	5-1	2-3	1-1	0-1	1-1	2-2	1-1	0-3	1-0	2-0	1-1	2-0	3-1		2-0	1-0	3-1	1-1	4-2	4-2	3-2
Newport County	3-0	2-0	4-1	3-1	0-1	1-2	0-1	4-0	3-1	3-4	4-2	1-0	2-0	5-1	1-1		4-3	3-1	1-3	3-1	1-0	4-1
Salisbury City	0-0	3-1	3-1	2-1	0-1	2-0	1-1	1-2	1-0	0-1	3-0	1-1	0-0	0-3	1-1	2-1		1-0	0-0	1-0	0-0	4-0
Sutton United	3-3	3-1	1-1	3-2	0-0	2-2	0-0	3-1	2-2	1-0	2-2	0-1	1-0	1-0	0-2	1-1	0-1		2-1	1-2	3-1	1-3
Thurrock	2-2	2-1	0-3	1-1	0-1	1-0	2-3	2-4	1-1	1-4	5-1	1-1	0-1	0-4	3-2	2-2	1-5	3-0		1-2	2-2	1-0
Welling United	0-2	5-0	2-3	3-0	4-1	1-0	1-2	1-0	2-1	1-0	2-0	1-1	1-1	2-4	0-0	2-3	1-2	1-0	1-2		1-0	5-1
Weston-super-Mare	1-3	2-1	1-2	1-3	0-0	0-1	1-2	2-4	3-3	2-1	0-1	1-5	0-5	1-2	1-1	3-4	1-1	0-2	2-1	1-2		2-1
Yeading	1-1	2-1	1-1	2-0	0-1	5-0	0-0	2-5	1-4	2-1	1-1	1-1	1-1	1-3	1-0	1-1	1-3	2-2	2-1	0-1	0-0	

Nationwide Conference South

Season 2006/2007

Histon	42	30	4	8	85	44	94
Salisbury City	42	21	12	9	65	37	75
Braintree Town	42	21	11	10	51	38	74
Havant & Waterlooville	42	20	13	9	75	46	73
Bishop's Stortford	42	21	10	11	72	61	73
Newport County	42	21	7	14	83	57	70
Eastbourne Borough	42	18	15	9	58	42	69
Welling United	42	21	6	15	65	51	69
Lewes	42	15	17	10	67	52	62
Fisher Athletic	42	15	11	16	77	77	56
Farnborough Town	42	19	8	15	59	52	55
Bognor Regis Town	42	13	13	16	56	62	52
Cambridge City	42	15	7	20	44	52	52
Sutton United	42	14	9	19	58	63	51
Eastleigh	42	11	15	16	48	53	48
Yeading	42	12	9	21	56	78	45
Dorchester Town	42	11	12	19	49	77	45
Thurrock	42	11	11	20	58	79	44
Basingstoke Town	42	9	16	17	46	58	43
Hayes	42	11	10	21	47	73	43
Weston-super-Mare	42	8	11	23	49	77	35
Bedford Town	42	8	7	27	43	82	31

Farnborough Town had 10 points deducted.

Promotion Play-offs South

Bishop's Stortford 1   Salisbury City 1
Havant & Waterlooville 1   Braintree Town 1

Salisbury City 3   Bishop's Stortford .... 1 (aet)
Salisbury City won 4-2 on aggregate
Braintree Town 1   Havant & Waterlooville .. 1 (aet)
Braintree Town won 4-2 on penalties

Braintree Town 0   Salisbury City 1

Promoted from Conference South: Histon and Salisbury City

Northern Premier League — Premier Division — 2006/2007 Season

	AFC Telford Utd	Ashton Utd	Burscough	Fleetwood Town	Frickley Athletic	Gateshead	Grantham Town	Guiseley	Hednesford Town	Ilkeston Town	Kendal Town	Leek Town	Lincoln United	Marine	Matlock Town	Mossley	North Ferriby Utd	Ossett Town	Prescot Cables	Radcliffe Borough	Whitby Town	Witton Albion
AFC Telford United	■	0-0	1-2	2-2	4-1	4-0	1-1	3-2	0-0	1-1	2-2	5-1	1-1	1-1	3-1	0-0	2-1	4-1	2-1	1-1	1-3	3-1
Ashton United	0-5	■	2-1	3-0	1-0	0-3	1-0	3-0	3-4	1-1	3-3	1-4	2-0	2-4	1-1	1-0	0-3	2-3	2-1	2-1	1-2	2-1
Burscough	0-0	3-2	■	4-1	5-2	2-0	3-0	1-0	2-0	1-1	8-2	2-0	0-2	0-0	0-0	4-0	3-2	4-0	1-0	2-2	4-0	1-0
Fleetwood Town	3-0	1-1	1-0	■	2-2	1-0	4-1	1-2	1-2	4-1	2-1	2-1	2-0	2-3	1-1	0-1	4-1	1-0	4-0	0-3	3-1	2-0
Frickley Athletic	0-1	2-0	1-2	1-3	■	1-1	1-1	2-0	0-2	0-2	2-1	3-1	2-0	1-2	2-0	0-4	1-1	0-0	1-1	2-2	3-2	2-1
Gateshead	4-3	2-3	1-0	3-3	2-3	■	5-2	0-1	2-3	2-1	1-1	2-1	2-2	2-0	3-2	2-0	0-0	2-1	2-3	3-1	0-0	1-0
Grantham Town	0-1	1-1	0-3	0-2	0-0	0-6	■	0-1	1-2	0-4	2-1	3-1	1-2	0-2	1-2	0-5	1-3	0-1	0-0	2-3	2-3	
Guiseley	0-1	2-1	1-1	1-1	5-1	1-1	2-0	■	1-1	3-3	2-1	1-2	1-1	3-1	2-1	5-1	1-1	1-2	3-1	2-1	5-0	1-3
Hednesford Town	0-1	0-0	2-2	2-1	2-1	1-1	2-0	2-2	■	3-0	2-1	1-0	2-1	0-2	1-2	0-0	1-1	1-1	1-0	0-0	3-0	0-1
Ilkeston Town	1-1	2-1	2-2	2-2	1-2	4-2	2-1	1-2	2-0	■	2-2	2-0	0-1	0-2	1-3	2-1	1-1	0-2	0-2	1-2	3-0	0-0
Kendal Town	1-1	2-1	1-3	4-1	2-0	1-1	2-0	0-3	2-3	0-3	■	0-1	0-1	0-2	1-5	3-1	1-0	0-0	3-3	3-1	1-0	1-5
Leek Town	0-1	1-0	1-1	1-2	0-1	0-2	4-2	1-1	2-1	2-1	0-1	■	0-1	2-1	1-0	1-2	1-0	0-3	1-1	0-0	2-2	1-2
Lincoln United	0-4	1-1	1-1	1-1	1-1	2-4	1-0	0-0	0-0	0-2	1-1	1-2	■	1-2	0-0	2-0	2-0	0-0	2-2	0-1	1-0	1-0
Marine	0-2	2-1	2-3	2-0	1-2	2-1	1-0	1-0	1-1	1-1	1-1	4-1		■	1-2	1-0	4-1	3-2	1-0	2-1	3-1	2-2
Matlock Town	2-1	0-0	1-3	1-1	3-0	0-0	3-2	0-3	0-1	5-1	1-0	2-0	1-2		■	4-1	2-0	1-0	3-0	3-2	5-1	1-1
Mossley	3-4	1-2	3-2	0-1	1-2	0-4	3-2	1-3	1-1	2-3	0-2	1-0	1-2	1-3	0-3	■	1-2	0-2	0-0	2-0	2-0	1-2
North Ferriby United	1-2	3-0	0-2	4-1	3-2	3-1	2-2	0-2	1-0	1-1	4-1	1-5	1-1	1-0	0-2	2-1	■	0-2	0-1	1-0	2-0	0-4
Ossett Town	0-0	2-1	0-0	2-4	2-0	2-2	2-2	1-0	0-1	1-2	2-1	2-0	1-3	1-1	2-1	3-2	1-2	■	2-1	4-0	2-2	1-2
Prescot Cables	0-1	1-0	1-2	3-1	1-1	1-1	2-1	2-0	0-0	1-4	2-2	2-2	3-0	2-1	1-3	2-2	0-0	2-1	■	3-0	0-1	1-1
Radcliffe Borough	1-1	2-0	1-0	0-2	1-0	0-2	2-1	1-2	0-1	1-3	1-3	0-0	3-3	3-3	1-1	1-3	0-2	0-2	1-1	■	2-4	0-2
Whitby Town	1-0	2-3	1-0	0-0	3-2	2-1	3-1	2-2	2-0	4-1	1-0	2-2	2-0	2-1	1-2	3-2	4-1	0-2	1-2	3-2	■	0-2
Witton Albion	0-1	5-1	0-0	3-1	2-0	1-1	4-4	2-2	3-0	4-1	1-3	3-4	6-0	5-2	1-0	2-1	2-0	3-1	2-1	1-0	7-2	■

Unibond League Premier Division

Season 2006/2007

	P	W	D	L	F	A	Pts
Burscough	42	23	12	7	80	37	80
Witton Albion	42	24	8	10	90	48	80
AFC Telford United	42	21	15	6	72	40	78
Marine	42	22	8	12	70	53	74
Matlock Town	42	21	9	12	70	43	72
Guiseley	42	19	12	11	71	49	69
Hednesford Town	42	18	14	10	49	41	68
Fleetwood Town	42	19	10	13	71	60	67
Gateshead	42	17	14	11	75	57	65
Ossett Town	42	18	10	14	61	52	64
Whitby Town	42	18	6	18	63	78	60
Ilkeston Town	42	16	11	15	66	62	59
North Ferriby United	42	15	9	18	54	61	54
Prescot Cables	42	13	14	15	52	56	53
Lincoln United	42	12	15	15	40	58	51
Frickley Athletic	42	13	10	19	50	69	49
Leek Town	42	13	9	20	49	61	48
Ashton United	42	13	9	20	52	72	48
Kendal Town	42	12	11	19	59	79	47
Mossley	42	10	5	27	48	79	35
Radcliffe Borough	42	7	11	24	39	71	32
Grantham Town	42	3	8	31	39	94	17

Burscough had one point deducted.

Promotion Play-offs

AFC Telford United 2   Marine 0

Witton Albion 4   Matlock Town .... 2 (aet)

North Ferriby United won 4-2 on penalties

Witton Albion 1   AFC Telford United 3

Promoted: Burscough and AFC Telford United

Southern League Premier Division 2006/2007 Season

	Banbury United	Bath City	Cheshunt	Chippenham Town	Cirencester Town	Clevedon Town	Corby Town	Gloucester City	Halesowen Town	Hemel Hempstead Town	Hitchin Town	King's Lynn	Maidenhead United	Mangotsfield United	Merthyr Tydfil	Northwood	Rugby Town	Stamford	Team Bath	Tiverton Town	Wealdstone	Yate Town
Banbury United		1-1	1-1	5-0	2-0	2-0	1-0	1-2	1-1	1-3	2-3	3-3	0-2	1-2	2-2	0-2	2-3	0-0	0-2	4-3	3-1	1-2
Bath City	1-0		5-0	1-0	1-0	0-3	3-1	2-2	3-0	1-0	1-2	1-1	2-1	2-0	4-0	0-0	6-0	1-2	5-0	1-1	2-1	1-1
Cheshunt	1-2	0-2		3-0	4-0	2-1	3-1	0-3	0-0	2-0	1-2	2-2	3-2	1-3	2-1	1-2	2-1	4-2	0-2	1-0	0-0	2-3
Chippenham Town	1-1	0-1	1-0		0-0	2-0	2-1	1-0	1-1	2-2	3-0	1-3	2-1	0-0	0-1	5-1	2-3	1-1	1-0	5-3	2-0	3-1
Cirencester Town	0-2	0-1	3-3	1-3		1-1	2-3	1-3	0-2	4-2	0-0	1-6	1-0	1-1	0-0	6-3	3-1	1-0	0-1	4-1	0-3	0-0
Clevedon Town	1-1	0-2	1-3	2-3	5-1		1-1	2-2	0-1	0-0	2-2	3-1	1-3	1-1	1-0	3-1	3-0	2-3	0-1	0-2	2-2	2-0
Corby Town	0-3	0-2	3-2	3-3	0-0	1-1		2-3	0-1	0-0	2-3	3-0	1-0	0-2	3-2	0-0	1-2	1-2	1-3	0-0	2-4	4-0
Gloucester City	1-4	0-4	0-2	1-0	0-0	3-1	2-0		1-3	3-4	1-1	0-2	2-1	1-2	3-3	3-3	3-2	1-1	2-2	1-0	0-3	
Halesowen Town	3-2	3-4	1-0	2-1	4-2	1-0	1-3	1-1		3-1	2-2	2-3	1-3	0-0	1-0	2-2	1-0	4-0	1-1	2-2	5-3	3-0
Hemel Hempstead Town	2-0	1-0	2-0	0-0	4-1	2-3	3-1	3-3	0-0		2-0	1-5	1-0	1-1	3-0	4-0	4-2	1-1	0-0	4-1	5-2	1-2
Hitchin Town	1-2	0-4	0-1	3-2	1-1	1-0	1-0	2-2	1-0	1-1		0-1	2-1	1-0	1-0	1-0	3-1	1-3	2-3	4-2	4-2	
King's Lynn	2-0	1-1	4-1	3-0	2-0	0-0	2-1	0-1	0-2	2-1	1-0		0-1	3-0	0-0	2-1	2-1	3-1	1-0	4-1	1-0	4-0
Maidenhead United	2-0	0-2	3-0	0-0	1-0	0-5	1-3	1-0	1-0	1-1	3-0	1-1		3-0	1-1	2-0	3-0	3-0	0-2	1-1	3-0	1-1
Mangotsfield United	2-3	0-0	2-2	0-2	1-1	0-0	1-0	3-4	1-0	0-2	2-2	0-0	0-0		2-2	0-0	1-0	1-1	1-1	1-0	3-1	0-1
Merthyr Tydfil	0-0	2-1	1-0	0-1	2-0	1-0	0-0	1-1	2-3	4-1	5-1	5-0	1-1	0-0		0-2	2-1	2-1	1-2	1-0	3-0	0-0
Northwood	1-2	1-1	2-4	2-1	0-2	0-2	1-3	0-2	0-0	0-3	2-0	1-2	0-2	0-1	0-1		3-1	3-3	2-2	1-3	1-2	3-0
Rugby Town	1-2	1-4	2-1	0-1	1-3	2-3	3-0	2-1	4-3	0-3	0-0	1-0	1-1	0-2	2-0	3-0		2-6	1-0	4-1	2-0	0-1
Stamford	0-1	2-3	2-0	1-3	1-2	3-0	0-1	3-2	2-0	4-1	2-0	1-0	0-2	1-0	2-1	1-1			1-1	2-1	2-2	0-0
Team Bath	3-0	1-2	0-0	4-1	4-1	3-1	3-2	2-1	2-0	1-3	1-0	2-1	0-2	3-0	1-2	1-0	2-1	0-0		1-1	2-1	3-0
Tiverton Town	3-0	0-0	1-0	0-1	3-1	3-0	2-1	1-3	1-1	3-4	2-1	1-0	0-1	2-3	1-0	0-2	1-1	1-3	0-3		2-1	3-0
Wealdstone	4-0	0-4	5-2	3-1	2-2	3-3	2-1	0-1	1-3	2-2	4-0	1-1	0-3	1-1	1-2	1-1	2-1	2-5	2-1	2-1		0-1
Yate Town	2-2	1-2	3-0	2-3	2-0	1-4	2-2	2-2	2-2	4-1	2-5	3-0	0-0	2-2	2-2	1-0	2-3	3-1	3-0	0-1	2-4	

Southern League Premier Division

Season 2006/2007

Team	P	W	D	L	F	A	Pts
Bath City	42	27	10	5	84	29	91
Team Bath	42	23	9	10	66	42	78
King's Lynn	42	22	10	10	69	40	76
Maidenhead United	42	20	10	12	58	36	70
Hemel Hempstead Town	42	19	12	11	79	60	69
Halesowen Town	42	18	13	11	66	53	67
Chippenham Town	42	19	9	14	61	56	66
Stamford	42	16	11	15	65	62	59
Mangotsfield United	42	13	19	10	44	45	58
Gloucester City	42	15	13	14	67	70	58
Hitchin Town	42	16	9	17	55	68	57
Merthyr Tydfil	42	14	14	14	47	46	56
Banbury United	42	15	10	17	60	64	55
Yate Town	42	14	12	16	59	71	54
Tiverton Town	42	14	8	20	56	67	50
Cheshunt	42	14	7	21	56	71	49
Rugby Town	42	15	4	23	58	79	49
Clevedon Town	42	12	12	18	60	61	48
Wealdstone	42	13	9	20	69	82	48
Corby Town	42	10	9	23	52	69	39
Cirencester Town	42	9	12	21	46	76	39
Northwood	42	8	10	24	44	74	34

Promotion Play-offs

Team Bath 3   Hemel Hempstead Town 1
King's Lynn 0   Maidenhead United 1

Team Bath 0   Maidenhead United 1

Promoted: Bath City and Maidenhead United

Isthmian League Premier Division 2006/2007 Season	AFC Wimbledon	Ashford Town (Middlesex)	Billericay Town	Boreham Wood	Bromley	Carshalton Athletic	Chelmsford City	East Thurrock United	Folkestone Invicta	Hampton & Richmond	Harrow Borough	Hendon	Heybridge Swifts	Horsham	Leyton	Margate	Ramsgate	Slough Town	Staines Town	Tonbridge Angels	Walton & Hersham	Worthing
AFC Wimbledon		2-1	3-2	1-1	3-2	2-0	1-2	4-0	4-0	0-1	4-2	3-0	1-1	0-0	1-0	0-0	0-0	9-0	1-1	2-3	3-1	1-1
Ashford Town (Middlesex)	1-2		0-1	1-1	2-0	2-2	2-3	0-2	2-1	1-2	1-0	2-0	3-2	1-2	2-2	1-1	4-1	1-1	1-1	1-2	3-0	3-0
Billericay Town	3-0	5-0		0-0	0-0	0-0	2-1	2-1	1-1	1-0	3-0	2-1	0-0	1-0	2-0	3-2	0-1	5-0	1-0	3-0	3-1	3-1
Boreham Wood	0-0	5-4	1-1		0-2	0-0	2-0	1-2	1-2	0-2	1-1	3-2	2-1	1-2	1-1	6-1	1-2	6-0	2-1	1-3	1-0	3-2
Bromley	1-3	5-1	1-0	1-1		2-1	2-1	2-0	1-2	3-2	3-2	1-1	0-1	0-3	4-1	1-3	1-0	4-0	2-1	3-0	4-2	3-3
Carshalton Athletic	1-2	1-1	3-2	1-0	1-1		0-3	1-1	1-1	0-1	3-1	1-3	0-2	1-3	2-0	1-1	4-0	5-1	0-4	1-0	3-0	1-1
Chelmsford City	0-3	2-1	2-2	2-0	1-1	5-1		2-1	3-0	4-0	3-2	1-0	1-1	5-0	2-2	1-3	4-0	5-0	7-3	3-2	7-0	3-1
East Thurrock United	0-4	3-0	0-4	2-0	1-5	0-0	1-1		0-3	0-2	0-2	1-2	1-3	0-2	3-0	0-3	0-1	4-1	4-1	0-1	1-0	1-2
Folkestone Invicta	0-1	3-1	3-3	1-4	0-0	2-4	1-0	3-2		1-1	0-1	1-0	0-0	0-1	1-3	1-5	0-2	0-0	1-2	0-2	4-3	1-0
Hampton & Richmond	2-0	1-1	0-0	2-5	0-4	1-1	1-3	3-0	1-0		1-0	3-1	2-2	1-1	2-0	3-2	1-4	4-2	3-2	2-2	2-0	4-2
Harrow Borough	0-1	2-0	5-2	2-3	2-1	1-2	0-3	5-4	0-2	1-2		1-2	2-0	2-0	1-1	4-4	1-3	0-2	1-2	0-1	1-0	1-0
Hendon	3-1	0-0	0-1	1-2	0-2	3-5	0-3	2-1	1-0	0-2	1-1		1-1	2-0	1-2	1-0	2-4	2-0	1-1	0-1	3-0	2-1
Heybridge Swifts	0-1	0-2	1-2	1-1	0-1	0-1	1-1	0-0	2-0	2-2	2-1	0-0		1-1	3-0	1-0	2-0	2-3	1-0	2-1	2-0	3-1
Horsham	1-1	1-1	3-1	0-2	1-1	1-1	2-1	1-1	2-2	1-2	1-4	4-1	1-1		2-1	0-4	4-1	4-0	1-1	4-3	4-0	1-1
Leyton	2-5	1-1	3-2	0-1	0-0	3-0	3-2	0-3	0-0	0-3	2-1	1-4	1-6	1-3		0-4	4-1	1-0	4-2	0-1	3-0	1-1
Margate	0-0	1-1	0-0	0-2	0-0	1-0	3-0	1-1	1-0	2-0	4-1	4-1	0-1	1-1	5-1		1-0	2-1	2-4	1-2	3-0	2-1
Ramsgate	1-1	2-1	2-0	1-1	1-3	2-1	1-1	3-0	3-0	1-3	2-0	3-0	2-0	0-2	0-3	1-1		2-1	1-0	2-3	1-0	4-3
Slough Town	0-0	0-2	2-0	0-4	0-8	0-2	0-4	0-5	0-2	0-3	0-5	0-1	0-2	1-3	0-1	2-2	0-3		0-2	2-3	0-5	1-1
Staines Town	1-1	2-2	0-1	2-1	1-4	3-1	1-1	2-3	1-0	2-2	1-1	1-3	2-1	0-0	1-1	1-0	3-1	1-2		2-0	2-0	2-2
Tonbridge Angels	1-3	4-1	1-2	1-1	1-2	2-0	3-1	1-3	3-3	1-3	1-0	3-1	2-3	1-4	2-5	1-2	3-2	3-2	3-1		0-0	6-1
Walton & Hersham	1-1	2-3	2-2	1-2	0-0	1-0	2-0	0-2	3-1	0-4	2-2	0-2	1-0	5-1	0-0	0-2	1-0	3-0	0-2	2-1		0-6
Worthing	1-1	3-1	1-3	0-1	1-2	0-0	0-2	0-2	1-2	1-1	1-2	1-2	0-3	3-2	2-1	2-5	3-2	2-2	1-2	1-0	2-0	

Rymans League Premier Division

Season 2006/2007

Hampton & Richmond	42	24	10	8	77	53	82
Bromley	42	23	11	8	83	43	80
Chelmsford City	42	23	8	11	96	51	77
Billericay Town	42	22	11	9	71	42	77
AFC Wimbledon	42	21	15	6	76	37	75
Margate	42	20	11	11	79	48	71
Boreham Wood	42	19	12	11	71	49	69
Horsham	42	18	14	10	70	57	68
Ramsgate	42	20	5	17	63	63	65
Heybridge Swifts	42	17	13	12	57	40	64
Tonbridge Angels	42	20	4	18	74	72	64
Staines Town	42	15	12	15	64	64	57
Carshalton Athletic	42	14	12	16	54	59	54
Hendon	42	16	6	20	53	64	54
Leyton	42	13	10	19	55	77	49
East Thurrock United	42	14	6	22	56	70	48
Ashford Town (Middlesex)	42	11	13	18	59	71	46
Folkestone Invicta	42	12	10	20	45	66	46
Harrow Borough	42	13	6	23	61	71	45
Worthing	42	8	11	23	57	82	35
Walton & Hersham	42	9	6	27	38	83	33
Slough Town	42	4	6	32	26	123	18

AFC Wimbledon had 3 points deducted.

Promotion Play-offs

Bromley 1   AFC Wimbledon 0
Chelmsford City 1   Billericay Town .... 1 (aet)
Billericay Town won 5-3 on penalties

Bromley 1   Billericay Town .... 1 (aet)
Billericay Town won 4-2 on penalties

Promoted: Hampton & Richmond Borough and Billericay Town

Johnstone's Paint Trophy 2006/2007

Round 1	Accrington Stanley	1	Carlisle United	1
	Accrington Stanley won on penalties			
Round 1	Bradford City	1	Scunthorpe United	2
Round 1	Brighton & Hove Albion	2	Boston United	0
Round 1	Bristol Rovers	1	Torquay United	0
Round 1	Bury	0	Tranmere Rovers	2
Round 1	Gillingham	1	Nottingham Forest	2
Round 1	Hartlepool United	3	Rotherham United	1
Round 1	Hereford United	1	Shrewsbury Town	2
Round 1	Huddersfield Town	1	Doncaster Rovers	2
Round 1	Lincoln City	0	Grimsby Town	0
	Grimsby Town won on penalties			
Round 1	Macclesfield Town	0	Stockport County	1
Round 1	Northampton Town	0	Brentford	0
	Brentford won on penalties			
Round 1	Notts County	0	Barnet	1
Round 1	Walsall	1	Swansea City	1
	Swansea City won on penalties			
Round 1	Wrexham	1	Rochdale	1
	Rochdale won on penalties			
Round 1	Wycombe Wanderers	1	Swindon Town	0
Round 2	Accrington Stanley	4	Blackpool	4
	Accrington Stanley won on penalties			
Round 2	Brighton & Hove Albion	4	MiltonKeynes Dons	1
Round 2	Cheltenham Town	3	Barnet	2
Round 2	Chester City	3	Stockport County	0
Round 2	Hartlepool United	1	Doncaster Rover	3
Round 2	Leyton Orient	1	Bristol City	3
Round 2	Mansfield Town	3	Grimsby Town	0
Round 2	Millwall	2	Bournemouth	0
Round 2	Nottingham Forest	2	Brentford	1
Round 2	Oldham Athletic	0	Chesterfield	1
Round 2	Peterborough United	1	Swansea City	0
Round 2	Rochdale	1	Crewe Alexandra	1
	Crewe Alexandra won on penalties			
Round 2	Scunthorpe United	0	Port Vale	0
	Port Vale won on penalties			
Round 2	Shrewsbury Town	2	Yeovil Town	1
Round 2	Tranmere Rovers	0	Darlington	1
Round 2	Wycombe Wanderers	0	Bristol Rovers	2
Round 3	Bristol Rovers	1	Peterborough United	0
Round 3	Cheltenham Town	2	Shrewsbury Town	3
Round 3	Chesterfield	4	Chester City	4
	Chesterfield won on penalties			
Round 3	Darlington	1	Mansfield Town	0
Round 3	Doncaster Rovers	2	Accrington Stanley	0
Round 3	Millwall	1	Brighton & Hove Albion	1
	Brighton & Hove Albion won on penalties			
Round 3	Nottingham Forest	2	Bristol City	2
	Bristol City won on penalties			
Round 3	Port Vale	2	Crewe Alexandra	3

Semi-Final North	Chesterfield	2	Crewe Alexandra	4	
Semi-Final North	Doncaster Rovers	2	Darlington	0	
Semi-Final South	Bristol City	2	Brighton & Hove Albion	0	
Semi-Final South	Shrewsbury Town	0	Bristol Rovers	1	

Southern Final

1st leg	Bristol City	0	Bristol Rovers	0	
2nd leg	Bristol Rovers	1	Bristol City	0	
	Bristol Rovers won 1-0 on aggregate				

Northern Final

1st leg	Crewe Alexandra	3	Doncaster Rovers	3	
2nd leg	Doncaster Rovers	3	Crewe Alexandra	2	
	Doncaster Rovers won 6-5 on aggregate				

FINAL	Doncaster Rovers	3	Bristol Rovers	2	(aet)

F.A. Trophy 2006/2007

Qualifying 1	AFC Hornchurch	1	Harrow Borough	0
Qualifying 1	AFC Sudbury	2	Kingstonian	2
Qualifying 1	AFC Telford United	1	Eastwood Town	1
Qualifying 1	AFC Wimbledon	2	Dunstable Town	1
Qualifying 1	Abingdon United	4	Bracknell Town	2
Qualifying 1	Alsager Town	3	Brigg Town	0
Qualifying 1	Ashford Town (Middx)	2	Brackley Town	1
Qualifying 1	Bath City	2	Bishop's Cleeve	1
Qualifying 1	Bedworth United	0	Solihull Borough	0
Qualifying 1	Billericay Town	2	Aylesbury United	2
Qualifying 1	Boreham Wood	1	Tooting & Mitcham United	1
Qualifying 1	Bridlington Town	2	Stamford	4
Qualifying 1	Bromley	6	East Thurrock United	3
Qualifying 1	Burnham	0	Team Bath	5
Qualifying 1	Burscough	2	Matlock Town	1
Qualifying 1	Carshalton Athletic	4	Potters Bar Town	1
Qualifying 1	Chasetown	3	Chorley	1
Qualifying 1	Chelmsford City	1	Maidstone United	2
Qualifying 1	Cheshunt	0	Cray Wanderers	1
Qualifying 1	Clevedon Town	1	Windsor & Eton	3
Qualifying 1	Corby Town	2	Hemel Hempstead	4
Qualifying 1	Dartford	6	Horsham YMCA	0
Qualifying 1	Evesham United	2	Brook House	0
Qualifying 1	Frickley Athletic	0	Cammell Laird	4
Qualifying 1	Guiseley	5	Grantham Town	4
Qualifying 1	Hampton & Richmond Borough	5	Hitchin Town	3
Qualifying 1	Hanwell Town	2	Rugby Town	1
Qualifying 1	Hastings United	0	Waltham Forest	1
Qualifying 1	Hednesford Town	2	Halesowen Town	2
Qualifying 1	Hendon	1	Ramsgate	2
Qualifying 1	Hillingdon Borough	2	Chippenham Town	2
Qualifying 1	Kendal Town	4	Buxton	2
Qualifying 1	Kidsgrove Athletic	2	Harrogate Railway	1
Qualifying 1	Leatherhead	1	Rothwell Town	0
Qualifying 1	Leighton Town	4	Slough Town	1
Qualifying 1	Maidenhead United	3	Dover Athletic	1
Qualifying 1	Maldon Town	0	Leyton	0
Qualifying 1	Marlow	0	Andover	0
Qualifying 1	Merthyr Tydfil	2	Stourbridge	0
Qualifying 1	Molesey	3	Barton Rovers	1
Qualifying 1	Mossley	5	Lincoln United	1
Qualifying 1	North Ferriby United	2	Bradford Park Avenue	2
Qualifying 1	Ossett Albion	2	Willenhall Town	2
Qualifying 1	Ossett Town	2	Ashton United	3
Qualifying 1	Paulton Rovers	0	Cirencester Town	3
Qualifying 1	Radcliffe Borough	3	Leek Town	2
Qualifying 1	Rushall Olympic	3	Colwyn Bay	0
Qualifying 1	Sittingbourne	0	Arlesey Town	0
Qualifying 1	Skelmersdale United	3	Prescot Cables	0
Qualifying 1	Spalding United	1	Ilkeston Town	4
Qualifying 1	Staines Town	0	Folkestone Invicta	1
Qualifying 1	Stourport Swifts	1	Mangotsfield United	5
Qualifying 1	Sutton Coldfield Town	2	Gateshead	2
Qualifying 1	Swindon Supermarine	2	Yate Town	1

Qualifying 1	Taunton Town	0	Banbury United	0
Qualifying 1	Thatcham Town	0	Didcot Town	3
Qualifying 1	Tilbury	0	Horsham	1
Qualifying 1	Tiverton Town	2	Gloucester City	2
Qualifying 1	Tonbridge Angels	3	Harlow Town	1
Qualifying 1	Waltham Abbey	1	Heybridge Swifts	1
Qualifying 1	Walton & Hersham	0	Great Wakering Rovers	1
Qualifying 1	Walton & Hersham	0	Great Wakering Rovers	1
Qualifying 1	Ware	0	Enfield	1
Qualifying 1	Warrington Town	0	Clitheroe	1
Qualifying 1	Wealdstone	2	Witham Town	0
Qualifying 1	Whitby Town	3	Shepshed Dynamo	0
Qualifying 1	Whyteleafe	0	Walton Casuals	0
Qualifying 1	Willenhall Town	2	Ossett Albion	1
Qualifying 1	Winchester City	1	Oxford City	0
Qualifying 1	Wingate & Finchley	0	Northwood	1
Qualifying 1	Witton Albion	2	Fleetwood Town	1
Qualifying 1	Wivenhoe Town	1	Margate	3
Qualifying 1	Woodley Sports	6	Marine	1
Qualifying 1	Worthing	0	King's Lynn	1
Replay	Andover	1	Marlow	2
Replay	Arlesey Town	1	Sittingbourne	2
Replay	Aylesbury United	1	Billericay Town	4
	Played at a neutral ground			
Replay	Banbury United	5	Taunton Town	1
Replay	Bradford Park Avenue	3	North Ferriby United	2
Replay	Chippenham Town	3	Hillingdon Borough	0 (aet)
Replay	Eastwood Town	1	AFC Telford United	0
Replay	Gateshead	3	Sutton Coldfield Town	0
Replay	Gloucester City	2	Tiverton Town	2 (aet)
	Gloucester City won on penalties			
Replay	Halesowen Town	2	Hednesford Town	1
Replay	Heybridge Swifts	8	Waltham Abbey	0
Replay	Kingstonian	2	AFC Sudbury	3
Replay	Leyton	3	Maldon Town	1
Replay	Solihull Borough	5	Bedworth United	1
Replay	Tooting & Mitcham United	2	Boreham Wood	0
Replay	Walton Casuals	5	Whyteleafe	0
Replay	Willenhall Town	2	Ossett Albion	1
Qualifying 2	AFC Hornchurch	1	Mangotsfield United	3
Qualifying 2	AFC Sudbury	2	Ramsgate	0
Qualifying 2	AFC Wimbledon	3	Tonbridge Angels	2
Qualifying 2	Ashton United	0	Gateshead	1
Qualifying 2	Bradford Park Avenue	2	Solihull Borough	0
Qualifying 2	Burscough	3	Eastwood Town	1
Qualifying 2	Cammell Laird	2	Mossley	1
Qualifying 2	Carshalton Athletic	0	Heybridge Swifts	1
Qualifying 2	Chippenham Town	3	Didcot Town	3
Qualifying 2	Dartford	0	Evesham United	1
Qualifying 2	Enfield	1	Walton Casuals	1
Qualifying 2	Folkestone Invicta	2	Billericay Town	3
Qualifying 2	Gloucester City	1	Margate	0
Qualifying 2	Great Wakering Rovers	0	Merthyr Tydfil	1
Qualifying 2	Halesowen Town	1	Clitheroe	1
Qualifying 2	Hanwell Town	2	Cirencester Town	3
Qualifying 2	Hemel Hempstead	8	Abingdon United	4

Qualifying 2	Ilkeston Town	2	Guiseley	0	
Qualifying 2	Kidsgrove Athletic	0	Chasetown	0	
Qualifying 2	Leatherhead	0	Team Bath	3	
Qualifying 2	Leighton Town	2	Wealdstone	2	
Qualifying 2	Leyton	1	King's Lynn	2	
Qualifying 2	Maidenhead United	2	Horsham	1	
Qualifying 2	Maidstone United	2	Ashford Town (Middx)	3	
Qualifying 2	Marlow	0	Banbury United	2	
Qualifying 2	Molesey	1	Swindon Supermarine	0	
Qualifying 2	Northwood	0	Winchester City	0	
Qualifying 2	Radcliffe Borough	1	Stamford	2	
Qualifying 2	Sittingbourne	0	Bath City	0	
Qualifying 2	Skelmersdale United	4	Kendal Town	2	
Qualifying 2	Tooting & Mitcham United	1	Bromley	1	
Qualifying 2	Waltham Forest	1	Cray Wanderers	2	
Qualifying 2	Willenhall Town	1	Rushall Olympic	1	
Qualifying 2	Windsor & Eton	2	Hampton & Richmond Borough	0	
Qualifying 2	Witton Albion	2	Alsager Town	0	
Qualifying 2	Woodley Sports	3	Whitby Town	2	
Replay	Bath City	4	Sittingbourne	0	
Replay	Bromley	0	Tooting & Mitcham United	1	
Replay	Chasetown	1	Kidsgrove Athletic	1	(aet)
	Chasetown won on penalties				
Replay	Clitheroe	1	Halesowen Town	0	
Replay	Didcot Town	3	Chippenham Town	1	(aet)
Replay	Rushall Olympic	2	Willenhall Town	0	
Replay	Walton Casuals	2	Enfield	2	(aet)
	Enfield won on penalties				
Replay	Wealdstone	3	Leighton Town	0	
Replay	Winchester City	1	Northwood	4	
Qualifying 3	AFC Wimbledon	1	Eastleigh	1	
Qualifying 3	Alfreton Town	0	Harrogate Town	1	
Qualifying 3	Ashford Town (Middx)	2	Thurrock	1	
Qualifying 3	Banbury United	2	Lewes	3	
Qualifying 3	Basingstoke Town	2	Bedford Town	0	
Qualifying 3	Bath City	1	Tooting & Mitcham United	1	
Qualifying 3	Billericay Town	1	Mangotsfield United	2	
Qualifying 3	Bishop's Stortford	2	Molesey	1	
Qualifying 3	Blyth Spartans	1	Worcester City	1	
Qualifying 3	Bradford Park Avenue	1	Nuneaton Borough	2	
Qualifying 3	Burscough	1	Scarborough	2	
Qualifying 3	Cambridge City	0	AFC Sudbury	1	
Qualifying 3	Chasetown	0	Hyde United	3	
Qualifying 3	Cray Wanderers	1	Yeading	1	
Qualifying 3	Didcot Town	0	Newport County	3	
Qualifying 3	Droylsden	3	Rushall Olympic	0	
Qualifying 3	Farnborough Town	1	Maidenhead United	1	
Qualifying 3	Gainsborough Trinity	1	Stalybridge Celtic	1	
Qualifying 3	Gloucester City	2	Eastbourne Borough	5	
Qualifying 3	Havant & Waterlooville	3	Team Bath	0	
Qualifying 3	Hayes	0	Fisher Athletic	5	
Qualifying 3	Hemel Hempstead	2	Evesham United	2	
Qualifying 3	Heybridge Swifts	2	Bognor Regis Town	0	
Qualifying 3	Hinckley United	1	Ilkeston Town	0	
Qualifying 3	Hucknall Town	1	Barrow	1	
Qualifying 3	Kettering Town	10	Clitheroe	1	

Qualifying 3	Lancaster City	0	Redditch United	1	
Qualifying 3	Leigh RMI	1	Cammell Laird	0	
Qualifying 3	Merthyr Tydfil	2	Wealdstone	1	
Qualifying 3	Moor Green	0	Woodley Sports	3	
Qualifying 3	Northwood	1	Histon	2	
Qualifying 3	Salisbury City	2	Enfield	1	
Qualifying 3	Skelmersdale United	1	Farsley Celtic	2	
Qualifying 3	Stamford	0	Witton Albion	3	
Qualifying 3	Sutton United	2	Braintree Town	3	
Qualifying 3	Tooting & Mitcham United	0	Bath City	1	
Qualifying 3	Vauxhall Motors (Cheshire)	2	Worksop Town	2	
Qualifying 3	Welling United	3	Dorchester Town	0	
Qualifying 3	Weston Super Mare	1	Cirencester Town	0	
Qualifying 3	Windsor & Eton	1	King's Lynn	2	
Qualifying 3	Workington	2	Gateshead	4	
Replay	Barrow	2	Hucknall Town	1	
Replay	Eastleigh	2	AFC Wimbledon	2	(aet)
	AFC Wimbledon won on penalties				
Replay	Evesham United	3	Hemel Hempstead	3	
Replay	Maidenhead United	0	Farnborough Town	3	
Replay	Stalybridge Celtic	2	Gainsborough Trinity	1	
Replay	Worcester City	1	Blyth Spartans	1	(aet)
	Worcester City won on penalties				
Replay	Worksop Town	0	Vauxhall Motors (Cheshire)	1	
Replay	Yeading	7	Cray Wanderers	1	
Round 1	Aldershot Town	1	AFC Wimbledon	2	
Round 1	Altrincham	0	Tamworth	0	
Round 1	Barrow	2	Worcester City	5	
Round 1	Bishop's Stortford	3	St Albans City	2	
Round 1	Braintree Town	3	Ashford Town (Middx)	0	
Round 1	Dagenham & Redbridge	2	Crawley Town	0	
Round 1	Exeter City	3	Heybridge Swifts	0	
Round 1	Farnborough Town	1	Bath City	1	
Round 1	Fisher Athletic	0	Eastbourne Borough	1	
Round 1	Forest Green Rovers	0	Yeading	1	
Round 1	Gateshead	0	Burton Albion	4	
Round 1	Halifax Town	3	Hyde United	1	
Round 1	Harrogate Town	1	Leigh RMI	1	
Round 1	Havant & Waterlooville	1	Gravesend & Northfleet	2	
Round 1	Histon	5	Cambridge United	0	
Round 1	Kettering Town	1	Stafford Rangers	0	
Round 1	Kidderminster Harriers	4	Vauxhall Motors (Cheshire)	4	
Round 1	Lewes	0	Oxford United	0	
Round 1	Mangotsfield United	2	King's Lynn	1	
Round 1	Morecambe	2	York City	1	
Round 1	Newport County	2	AFC Sudbury	1	
Round 1	Northwich Victoria	3	Farsley Celtic	1	
Round 1	Nuneaton Borough	0	Redditch United	3	
Round 1	Rushden & Diamonds	3	Scarborough	2	
Round 1	Salisbury City	3	Woking	1	
Round 1	Southport	1	Droylsden	0	
Round 1	Stalybridge Celtic	2	Hinckley United	2	
Round 1	Stevenage Borough	7	Merthyr Tydfil	0	
Round 1	Welling United	0	Basingstoke Town	0	
Round 1	Weston Super Mare	1	Evesham United	0	
Round 1	Weymouth	1	Grays Athletic	2	
Round 1	Woodley Sports	1	Witton Albion	3	

Replay	Basingstoke Town	0	Welling United	2	
Replay	Bath City	0	Farnborough Town	1	(aet)
Replay	Hinckley United	1	Stalybridge Celtic	2	
Replay	Leigh RMI	2	Harrogate Town	1	
Replay	Oxford United	1	Lewes	0	
Replay	Tamworth	2	Altrincham	1	
Replay	Vauxhall Motors (Cheshire)	0	Kidderminster Harriers	4	
Round 2	Eastbourne Borough	0	Northwich Victoria	1	
	Played at a neutral ground				
Round 2	Gravesend & Northfleet	0	AFC Wimbledon	1	
	AFC Wimbledon were disqualified after fielding an ineligible player				
Round 2	Exeter City	0	Kidderminster Harriers	1	
Round 2	Farnborough Town	0	Braintree Town	2	
Round 2	Morecambe	5	Mangotsfield United	0	
Round 2	Newport County	0	Histon	0	
Round 2	Oxford United	2	Halifax Town	2	
Round 2	Redditch United	3	Dagenham & Redbridge	2	
Round 2	Salisbury City	2	Southport	1	
Round 2	Stalybridge Celtic	1	Kettering Town	1	
Round 2	Stevenage Borough	3	Leigh RMI	1	
Round 2	Tamworth	1	Welling United	1	
Round 2	Weston Super Mare	0	Grays Athletic	4	
Round 2	Witton Albion	0	Rushden & Diamonds	1	
Round 2	Worcester City	2	Burton Albion	1	
Round 2	Yeading	2	Bishop's Stortford	0	
Replay	Halifax Town	2	Oxford United	1	
Replay	Histon	3	Newport County	1	
Replay	Kettering Town	3	Stalybridge Celtic	1	
Replay	Welling United	2	Tamworth	1	
	Played at a neutral ground				
Round 3	Gravesend & Northfleet	2	Rushden & Diamonds	1	
Round 3	Grays Athletic	2	Yeading	1	
Round 3	Halifax Town	3	Redditch United	1	
Round 3	Histon	1	Northwich Victoria	2	
Round 3	Kettering Town	0	Salisbury City	2	
Round 3	Kidderminster Harriers	0	Braintree Town	0	
Round 3	Morecambe	1	Stevenage Borough	1	
Round 3	Welling United	2	Worcester City	1	
Replay	Braintree Town	1	Kidderminster Harriers	3	
Replay	Stevenage Borough	3	Morecambe	0	(aet)
Round 4	Kidderminster Harriers	3	Halifax Town	1	
Round 4	Northwich Victoria	3	Gravesend & Northfleet	0	
Round 4	Stevenage Borough	3	Salisbury City	0	
Round 4	Welling United	1	Grays Athletic	4	
Semi-Finals					
1st leg	Kidderminster Harriers	2	Northwich Victoria	0	
2nd leg	Northwich Victoria	3	Kidderminster Harriers	2	
	Kidderminster Harriers won 4-3 on aggregate				
1st leg	Grays Athletic	0	Stevenage Borough	1	
2nd leg	Stevenage Borough	2	Grays Athletic	1	(aet)
	Stevenage Borough won 3-1 on aggregate				
FINAL	Stevenage Borough	3	Kidderminster Harriers	2	N

F.A. Vase 2006/2007

Round 1	AFC Totton	4	Chipping Norton Town	0	
Round 1	Alvechurch	1	Coleshill Town	0	
Round 1	Amesbury Town	4	Thame United	2	
Round 1	Ashington	1	Durham City	3	
Round 1	Atherstone Town	0	Boldmere St Michaels	1	
Round 1	Atherton Collieries	4	Winsford United	0	
Round 1	Banstead Athletic	3	Wealden	0	
Round 1	Barking	0	Hounslow Borough	4	
Round 1	Barwell	2	Mickleover Sports	0	
Round 1	Bedford United & Valerio	2	Cockfosters	1	
Round 1	Bemerton Heath Harlequins	4	Shrewton United	1	
Round 1	Biddulph Victoria	4	Shawbury United	1	
Round 1	Bideford	1	Welton Rovers	0	
Round 1	Billingham Town	0	Whitley Bay	1	
Round 1	Birstall United	0	Oldbury United	1	
Round 1	Bishop Auckland	1	Dunston Federation Brewery	2	
Round 1	Borrowash Victoria	0	Castle Vale	3	
Round 1	Boston Town	6	Bourne Town	0	
Round 1	Bristol Manor Farm	2	Bridport	0	
Round 1	Calne Town	4	Pewsey Vale	3	(aet)
Round 1	Calverton Miners Welfare	0	Newcastle Town	7	
Round 1	Causeway United	3	Tipton Town	2	
Round 1	Chipstead	0	Ash United	1	
Round 1	Clanfield 85	0	Chalfont St Peter	5	
Round 1	Cogenhoe United	3	Bowers & Pitsea	1	
Round 1	Colliers Wood United	2	Crowborough Athletic	1	
Round 1	Congleton Town	4	Dinnington Town	0	
Round 1	Corsham Town	1	Harefield United	0	
Round 1	Croydon	4	Littlehampton Town	0	
Round 1	Downes Sports	0	Holwell Sports	2	
Round 1	Eastbourne Town	3	Merstham	2	(aet)
Round 1	Eccleshill United	0	Newcastle Blue Star	3	
Round 1	Edgware Town	3	Brentwood Town	1	
Round 1	Egham Town	0	Whitehawk	2	
Round 1	Ely City	0	Wisbech Town	0	(aet)
Round 1	Erith & Belvedere	4	Cobham	1	
Round 1	Erith Town	2	Romford	3	
Round 1	Eton Manor	w.o.	Clapton		
	Clapton were disqualified before the game was played				
Round 1	Fakenham Town	5	Gorleston	0	
Round 1	Fareham Town	4	Ardley United	0	
Round 1	Feltham	0	Brimsdown Rovers	4	
Round 1	Flixton	3	Abbey Hey	1	
Round 1	Friar Lane & Epworth	0	Carlton Town	4	
Round 1	Garforth Town	3	Silsden	0	
Round 1	Glasshoughton Welfare	3	Easington Colliery	1	
Round 1	Guildford City	0	Three Bridges	2	
Round 1	Hailsham Town	4	Haywards Heath Town	1	
Round 1	Hall Road Rangers	1	Winterton Rangers	2	
Round 1	Hamble ASSC	0	Cowes Sports	5	
Round 1	Harpenden Town	2	Halstead Town	3	(aet)
Round 1	Holbrook Miners Welfare	2	Coalville Town	6	
Round 1	Horley Town	1	Sevenoaks Town	2	
Round 1	Ilfracombe Town	2	Hallen	1	

Round 1	Ipswich Wanderers	4	Soham Town Rangers	0	
Round 1	Kirkley	3	Godmanchester Rovers	0	
Round 1	Launceston	2	Liskeard Athletic	1	
Round 1	Leiston	0	Woodbridge Town	1	
Round 1	Liversedge	1	Norton & Stockton Ancients	0	
Round 1	Lymington Town	0	Shrivenham	0	(aet)
Round 1	Market Drayton Town	1	Quorn	2	
Round 1	Moneyfields	2	Sandhurst Town	2	(aet)
Round 1	Nelson	0	Sheffield	1	
Round 1	New Mills	2	Stratford Town	2	(aet)
Round 1	North Leigh	2	Milton United	1	(aet)
Round 1	North Shields	1	Consett	4	
Round 1	Oxhey Jets	3	Bedfont Green	2	
Round 1	Padiham	0	FC United Of Manchester	3	
Round 1	Poole Town	1	Frome Town	3	
Round 1	Porthleven	1	Bodmin Town	0	
Round 1	Potton United	2	Barkingside	1	
Round 1	Poulton Victoria	2	Curzon Ashton	2	
Round 1	Radcliffe Olympic	0	Rainworth MW	1	
Round 1	Reading Town	0	Gosport Borough	0	(aet)
Round 1	Retford United	2	Bolehall Swifts	2	(aet)
Round 1	Ringmer	0	Selsey	1	(aet)
Round 1	Romulus	1	Shifnal Town	0	
Round 1	Ryton	0	Billingham Synthonia	2	
Round 1	Saffron Walden Town	2	Thamesmead Town	1	
Round 1	Salford City	2	Blackpool Mechanics	1	
Round 1	Sherborne Town	2	Bishop Sutton	0	
Round 1	Sidley United	3	Arundel	2	
Round 1	Slimbridge	4	Barnstaple Town	0	
Round 1	South Normanton Athletic	4	Loughborough Dynamo	1	
Round 1	South Shields	2	Jarrow Roofing Boldon CA	1	
Round 1	St Neots Town	2	Blackstones	1	
Round 1	Stanway Rovers	2	Burnham Ramblers	2	(aet)
Round 1	Street	5	Penryn Athletic	2	
Round 1	Sunderland Nissan	3	Shildon	4	
Round 1	Sutton Town	2	Brierley & Hagley	2	(aet)
Round 1	Team Northumbria	0	West Auckland Town	3	
Round 1	Thetford Town	3	Lincoln Moorlands	2	
Round 1	Tiptree United	1	Ruislip Manor	3	(aet)
Round 1	Tividale	2	Barnt Green Spartak	1	
Round 1	Trafford	3	Parkgate	3	(aet)
Round 1	Truro City	2	Bitton	1	
Round 1	Tunbridge Wells	6	Pagham	1	
Round 1	Wantage Town	2	Witney United	1	
Round 1	Wellingborough Town	0	Leverstock Green	4	
Round 1	Wembley	1	Northampton Spencer	1	(aet)
Round 1	Wick	2	Oakwood	1	
Round 1	Willand Rovers	1	Odd Down	2	
Round 1	Worsbrough Bridge MW	2	Colne	4	
Round 1	Wroxham	4	Deeping Rangers	1	
Replay	Bolehall Swifts	0	Retford United	8	
Replay	Brierley & Hagley	0	Sutton Town	3	
Replay	Burnham Ramblers	0	Stanway Rovers	0	(aet)
	Burnham Ramblers won on penalties				
Replay	Curzon Ashton	3	Poulton Victoria	1	(aet)
Replay	Gosport Borough	5	Reading Town	0	

Replay	Northampton Spencer	1	Wembley	0	
Replay	Parkgate	2	Trafford	1	
Replay	Sandhurst Town	0	Moneyfields	1	
Replay	Shrivenham	1	Lymington Town	2	
Replay	Stratford Town	2	New Mills	1	(aet)
Replay	Wisbech Town	2	Ely City	1	(aet)
Round 2	AFC Totton	4	Gosport Borough	1	
Round 2	Amesbury Town	2	Corsham Town	5	
Round 2	Banstead Athletic	1	Colliers Wood United	2	(aet)
Round 2	Barwell	2	Arnold Town	1	
Round 2	Bedford United & Valerio	1	Welwyn Garden City	5	
Round 2	Bedlington Terriers	0	West Auckland Town	6	
Round 2	Bemerton Heath Harlequins	2	Porthleven	1	
Round 2	Biddulph Victoria	1	Alvechurch	3	
Round 2	Bideford	2	Tavistock	0	
Round 2	Billingham Synthonia	3	Colne	2	
Round 2	Boldmere St Michaels	0	Quorn	1	
Round 2	Brimsdown Rovers	2	Ipswich Wanderers	3	
Round 2	Bristol Manor Farm	0	Slimbridge	5	
Round 2	Brockenhurst	1	Sherborne Town	3	
Round 2	Broxbourne Borough V&E	1	Mildenhall Town	3	
Round 2	Burnham Ramblers	3	Hounslow Borough	2	
Round 2	Calne Town	2	Odd Down	1	(aet)
Round 2	Carlton Town	1	Coalville Town	2	
Round 2	Castle Vale	3	South Normanton Athletic	0	
Round 2	Causeway United	1	Holwell Sports	1	(aet)
Round 2	Chalfont St Peter	w.o.	Fareham Town		
	Fareham Town were disqualified for fielding an ineligible player				
Round 2	Chessington & Hook United	3	Erith & Belvedere	1	
Round 2	Congleton Town	1	Whitley Bay	3	
Round 2	Consett	3	Garforth Town	0	
Round 2	Croydon	3	Sidley United	1	
Round 2	Curzon Ashton	7	Parkgate	1	
Round 2	Dorking	1	Wick	2	
Round 2	Dunston Federation Brewery	1	Newcastle Benfield Bay Plastics	6	
Round 2	Durham City	1	Sheffield	0	
	Played at a neutral ground				
Round 2	Edgware Town	3	Saffron Walden Town	0	
Round 2	Fakenham Town	1	Newmarket Town	0	
Round 2	Flixton	4	Pickering Town	0	
Round 2	Glasshoughton Welfare	2	Atherton Collieries	1	
Round 2	Hailsham Town	2	Hythe Town	0	
Round 2	Halstead Town	5	Eton Manor	0	
Round 2	Ilfracombe Town	2	Wimborne Town	3	
Round 2	Kirkley	1	Cogenhoe United	2	
Round 2	Leamington	4	Sutton Town	0	
Round 2	Leverstock Green	1	Woodbridge Town	0	(aet)
Round 2	Lymington Town	1	Frome Town	0	
Round 2	Moneyfields	1	Cowes Sports	0	
Round 2	Nantwich Town	3	Shildon	4	(aet)
Round 2	Newcastle Blue Star	2	Liversedge	0	
Round 2	Newcastle Town	0	Gedling Town	2	
Round 2	North Leigh	2	Eastbourne Town	3	(aet)
Round 2	Northampton Spencer	5	Thetford Town	2	
Round 2	Potton United	3	Ruislip Manor	3	
Round 2	Retford United	2	Rainworth MW	1	

Round	Home	Score	Away	Score	Note
Round 2	Romford	4	Oxhey Jets	4	(aet)
Round 2	Romulus	3	Oldbury United	1	
Round 2	Salford City	2	FC United Of Manchester	3	
	Played at a neutral ground				
Round 2	Selsey	3	Wantage Town	0	
Round 2	South Shields	5	Crook Town	4	(aet)
Round 2	St Neots Town	1	Lowestoft Town	6	
Round 2	Stratford Town	2	Tividale	0	(aet)
Round 2	Street	3	Launceston	3	(aet)
Round 2	Thackley	3	Squires Gate	2	
Round 2	Three Bridges	2	Sevenoaks Town	0	
Round 2	Truro City	3	St Blazey	2	
Round 2	VCD Athletic	3	Tunbridge Wells	0	
Round 2	Whitehawk	3	Ash United	0	(aet)
Round 2	Winterton Rangers	3	Ashville	1	
Round 2	Wisbech Town	4	Boston Town	0	
Round 2	Wroxham	2	Needham Market	1	
Replay	Holwell Sports	0	Causeway United	3	
Replay	Launceston	4	Street	4	(aet)
	Street won on penalties				
Replay	Oxhey Jets	3	Romford	1	
Replay	Ruislip Manor	1	Potton United	2	
Round 3	AFC Totton	3	Moneyfields	0	
Round 3	Barwell	4	Thackley	2	
Round 3	Bideford	3	Corsham Town	1	
Round 3	Billingham Synthonia	5	Romulus	2	
Round 3	Burnham Ramblers	3	Wroxham	1	
Round 3	Calne Town	1	Slimbridge	4	
Round 3	Chalfont St Peter	0	Wimborne Town	2	(aet)
Round 3	Chessington & Hook United	0	Street	4	
Round 3	Consett	2	Causeway United	3	
Round 3	Croydon	0	Leamington	1	
Round 3	Durham City	1	Flixton	4	
Round 3	FC United Of Manchester	2	Quorn	3	(aet)
Round 3	Fakenham Town	1	Cogenhoe United	5	
Round 3	Gedling Town	0	West Auckland Town	2	
Round 3	Glasshoughton Welfare	4	Winterton Rangers	3	
Round 3	Hailsham Town	2	Sherborne Town	4	(aet)
Round 3	Halstead Town	0	Edgware Town	1	
Round 3	Ipswich Wanderers	4	Oxhey Jets	0	
Round 3	Leverstock Green	0	Potton United	1	
Round 3	Lowestoft Town	5	Welwyn Garden City	0	
Round 3	Lymington Town	0	Truro City	1	
Round 3	Mildenhall Town	2	Northampton Spencer	1	
Round 3	Newcastle Benfield Bay Plastics	2	Castle Vale	0	
Round 3	Newcastle Blue Star	3	Alvechurch	2	
Round 3	Retford United	4	Shildon	3	
Round 3	South Shields	3	Curzon Ashton	4	
Round 3	Stratford Town	2	Colliers Wood United	1	(aet)
Round 3	Three Bridges	1	Bemerton Heath Harlequins	1	(aet)
Round 3	Whitehawk	2	Selsey	0	
Round 3	Whitley Bay	1	Coalville Town	0	
Round 3	Wick	0	Eastbourne Town	1	
Round 3	Wisbech Town	1	VCD Athletic	2	
Replay	Bemerton Heath Harlequins	3	Three Bridges	0	0

Round 4	Bideford	7	Barwell	0	
Round 4	Billingham Synthonia	2	Newcastle Blue Star	0	
Round 4	Burnham Ramblers	1	Street	2	
Round 4	Causeway United	2	Cogenhoe United	1	(aet)
Round 4	Eastbourne Town	0	Curzon Ashton	3	
Round 4	Flixton	2	Retford United	5	
Round 4	Leamington	4	Bemerton Heath Harlequins	1	
Round 4	Lowestoft Town	1	Ipswich Wanderers	2	(aet)
Round 4	Mildenhall Town	2	Sherborne Town	1	
Round 4	Potton United	1	AFC Totton	2	
Round 4	Quorn	2	Stratford Town	1	
Round 4	Slimbridge	1	Whitley Bay	0	
Round 4	Truro City	3	Newcastle Benfield Bay Plastics	1	
Round 4	VCD Athletic	2	West Auckland Town	1	
Round 4	Whitehawk	1	Edgware Town	1	(aet)
Round 4	Wimborne Town	4	Glasshoughton Welfare	2	(aet)
Replay	Edgware Town	0	Whitehawk	1	
Round 5	Billingham Synthonia	4	Mildenhall Town	0	
Round 5	Causeway United	0	Curzon Ashton	5	
Round 5	Ipswich Wanderers	1	AFC Totton	2	
Round 5	Leamington	5	Retford United	1	
Round 5	Slimbridge	0	Truro City	3	
Round 5	VCD Athletic	2	Bideford	3	
Round 5	Whitehawk	2	Quorn	1	
Round 5	Wimborne Town	4	Street	0	
Round 6	AFC Totton	2	Wimborne Town	1	(aet)
Round 6	Billingham Synthonia	1	Bideford	0	
Round 6	Curzon Ashton	4	Leamington	1	
Round 6	Whitehawk	0	Truro City	1	

Semi-Finals

1st leg	AFC Totton	1	Billingham Synthonia	2	
2nd leg	Billingham Synthonia	1	AFC Totton	2	(aet)
	AFC Totton won on penalties				
1st leg	Curzon Ashton	1	Truro City	0	
2nd leg	Truro City	3	Curzon Ashton	1	

| **FINAL** | AFC Totton | 1 | Truro City | 3 | |

	Aldershot Town	Altrincham	Burton Albion	Cambridge United	Crawley Town	Droylsden	Ebbsfleet United	Exeter City	Farsley Celtic	Forest Green Rovers	Grays Athletic	Halifax Town	Histon	Kidderminster Harriers	Northwich Victoria	Oxford United	Rushden & Diamonds	Salisbury City	Stafford Rangers	Stevenage Borough	Torquay United	Weymouth	Woking	York City
Aldershot Town		22/03	12/04	12/02	27/08	18/08	09/10	29/09	22/09	19/01	24/11	20/10	15/03	01/03	08/09	02/02	17/11	05/04	08/12	16/02	14/08	26/04	01/01	18/09
Altrincham	01/09		09/10	18/09	23/02	22/09	20/10	11/08	12/02	08/03	25/08	04/03	26/04	01/12	26/12	08/09	06/10	12/04	24/03	29/12	29/03	17/11	02/02	19/01
Burton Albion	13/10	08/04		24/11	22/03	12/02	18/09	03/05	27/08	08/12	05/04	23/02	01/03	03/11	19/01	18/08	02/02	06/10	01/01	19/04	08/09	15/03	22/09	14/08
Cambridge United	25/09	26/01	29/12		15/09	01/12	27/08	05/01	18/08	23/02	04/09	06/10	26/12	29/03	17/11	14/08	09/10	20/10	12/04	09/02	26/04	22/03	15/03	01/03
Crawley Town	24/03	29/09	01/09	02/02		08/09	12/02	04/03	24/11	22/09	08/12	26/04	09/10	16/02	25/08	01/01	19/01	08/03	20/10	11/08	17/11	12/04	18/09	05/04
Droylsden	08/03	09/02	25/09	05/04	05/01		12/04	25/08	09/10	24/11	01/09	24/03	20/10	26/01	04/03	06/10	08/12	11/08	17/11	04/09	23/02	15/09	26/04	01/01
Ebbsfleet United	08/04	19/04	26/01	24/03	25/09	13/10		09/02	23/02	03/11	01/01	25/08	04/09	15/09	11/08	03/05	08/03	04/03	24/11	01/09	06/10	05/01	05/04	08/12
Exeter City	23/02	01/03	17/11	08/09	14/08	15/03	22/09		02/02	18/09	06/10	29/03	29/12	22/03	12/04	19/01	20/10	09/10	26/04	01/12	26/12	27/08	12/02	18/08
Farsley Celtic	09/02	25/09	24/03	08/03	29/12	08/04	29/09	15/09		19/04	03/05	26/12	05/01	04/09	01/09	13/10	04/03	25/08	11/08	26/01	01/12	29/03	16/02	03/11
Forest Green Rovers	04/09	18/08	29/03	29/09	09/02	29/12	26/04	26/01	20/10		05/01	01/12	17/11	26/12	09/10	01/03	12/04	15/09	16/02	25/09	27/08	14/08	22/03	15/03
Grays Athletic	29/12	15/03	01/12	19/01	29/03	22/03	26/12	16/02	17/11	08/09		12/04	27/08	18/08	20/10	18/09	12/02	26/04	02/02	29/09	01/03	09/10	14/08	22/09
Halifax Town	19/04	14/08	29/09	16/02	03/11	27/08	15/03	08/12	01/01	05/04	13/10		18/08	08/04	18/09	22/03	22/09	24/11	19/01	03/05	02/02	01/03	08/09	12/02
Histon	24/08	03/11	11/08	01/01	08/04	19/04	19/01	24/11	08/09	03/05	24/03	08/03		13/10	02/02	21/09	05/04	01/09	12/02	04/03	18/09	29/09	08/12	16/02
Kidderminster Harriers	11/08	05/04	26/04	08/12	06/10	18/09	02/02	01/09	19/01	01/01	08/03	09/10	12/04		12/02	24/11	24/03	23/02	04/03	25/08	22/09	20/10	17/11	08/09
Northwich Victoria	05/01	01/01	04/09	03/05	15/03	14/08	01/03	13/10	22/03	08/04	19/04	26/01	15/09	25/09		08/12	24/11	09/02	05/04	03/11	18/08	16/02	29/09	27/08
Oxford United	15/09	05/01	08/03	04/03	26/12	16/02	17/11	04/09	12/04	11/08	26/01	01/09	09/02	29/12	29/03		26/04	25/09	25/08	24/03	09/10	01/12	20/10	29/09
Rushden & Diamonds	03/05	16/02	15/09	08/04	04/09	29/03	18/08	19/04	14/08	13/10	25/09	09/02	01/12	27/08	29/12	03/11		05/01	29/09	26/12	15/03	26/01	01/03	22/03
Salisbury City	01/12	13/10	16/02	19/04	18/08	01/03	14/08	08/04	15/03	02/02	03/11	29/12	22/03	29/09	22/09	12/02	08/09		18/09	29/03	19/01	26/12	27/08	03/05
Stafford Rangers	29/03	27/08	26/12	13/10	19/04	03/05	29/12	03/11	01/03	06/10	15/09	04/09	25/09	14/08	01/12	15/03	23/02	26/01		05/01	22/03	09/02	18/08	08/04
Stevenage Borough	06/10	24/11	20/10	22/09	01/03	19/01	22/03	05/04	18/09	12/02	23/02	17/11	14/08	15/03	26/04	27/08	01/01	08/12	08/09		12/04	18/08	09/10	02/02
Torquay United	04/03	08/12	05/01	03/11	03/05	29/09	16/02	01/01	05/04	24/03	11/08	15/09	26/01	09/02	08/03	08/04	25/08	04/09	01/09	13/10		25/09	24/11	19/04
Weymouth	03/11	03/05	25/08	31/08	12/10	02/02	08/09	24/03	08/12	04/03	08/04	11/08	23/02	19/04	06/10	05/04	18/09	01/01	22/09	08/03	12/02		19/01	24/11
Woking	26/12	15/09	09/02	25/08	26/01	03/11	01/12	25/09	06/10	01/09	04/03	05/01	29/03	03/05	23/02	19/04	11/08	24/03	08/03	08/04	29/12	04/09		13/10
York City	26/01	04/09	04/03	11/08	01/12	26/12	29/03	08/03	26/04	25/08	09/02	25/09	06/10	05/01	24/03	23/02	01/09	17/11	09/10	15/09	20/10	29/12	12/04	

Football Conference Blue Square North Fixtures 2007/2008	AFC Telford	Alfreton Town	Barrow	Blyth Spartans	Boston United	Burscough	Gainsborough Trinity	Harrogate Town	Hinckley United	Hucknall Town	Hyde United	Kettering Town	Leigh RMI	Nuneaton Borough	Redditch United	Solihull Moors	Southport	Stafford Rangers	Tamworth	Vauxhall Motors	Worcester City	Workington
AFC Telford		18/09	29/03	01/12	18/08	06/10	01/09	12/04	01/03	26/01	16/02	10/11	19/01	22/12	15/03	14/08	22/03	27/10	01/01	26/04	27/08	05/01
Alfreton Town	23/02		09/02	22/12	27/08	12/04	01/12	15/09	03/05	01/01	29/03	26/01	10/11	14/08	19/04	22/03	18/08	05/01	27/10	08/03	22/09	20/10
Barrow	17/11	05/04		23/02	22/12	27/10	12/01	18/09	03/11	18/08	22/03	08/12	14/08	06/10	02/02	08/03	27/08	26/01	19/04	01/01	03/05	07/09
Blyth Spartans	15/09	11/08	23/10		12/01	18/09	26/01	26/12	24/03	15/03	25/08	29/03	27/10	08/12	10/11	26/04	09/02	01/03	01/09	06/10	12/04	29/12
Boston United	09/02	29/12	01/09	19/04		15/03	26/12	01/03	25/08	27/10	03/05	24/03	05/01	19/01	15/09	16/02	01/12	05/04	19/09	10/11	06/10	11/08
Burscough	03/05	02/02	05/01	22/03	22/09		19/04	10/11	20/10	08/09	08/03	01/12	26/02	09/02	05/04	19/01	01/01	14/08	22/12	27/08	18/08	23/10
Gainsborough Trinity	08/03	06/10	26/04	14/08	01/01	03/11		23/02	02/02	27/08	09/09	27/10	12/04	29/03	18/09	22/12	05/01	18/08	22/03	19/01	17/11	08/12
Harrogate Town	20/10	03/11	19/01	01/01	14/08	26/01	22/09		05/04	19/04	27/08	16/02	22/03	08/03	01/12	18/08	23/10	09/02	17/11	08/09	22/12	03/05
Hinckley United	08/09	08/12	16/02	18/08	26/01	29/03	10/11	06/10		22/03	12/04	17/09	08/03	01/01	27/10	27/08	23/02	26/04	12/01	22/12	13/08	17/11
Hucknall Town	11/08	26/12	24/03	20/10	08/03	26/04	29/12	02/02	15/09		17/11	12/01	29/03	12/04	25/08	10/11	19/01	23/02	08/12	22/09	23/10	01/09
Hyde United	22/09	19/01	20/10	05/01	02/02	15/09	24/03	29/12	01/12	01/03		15/03	09/02	26/04	01/09	27/10	10/11	26/12	18/08	13/08	23/02	05/04
Kettering Town	05/04	17/11	22/09	03/11	08/09	23/02	03/05	05/01	09/02	13/08	06/10		22/12	22/03	22/10	01/01	02/02	19/01	27/08	18/08	08/03	19/04
Leigh RMI	08/12	15/03	01/03	03/05	03/11	24/03	16/02	25/08	11/08	18/09	23/10	01/09		17/11	12/01	06/10	07/09	29/12	05/04	26/01	19/04	26/12
Nuneaton Borough	24/03	01/03	15/03	05/04	23/10	25/08	15/09	11/08	26/12	05/01	03/11	20/10	22/09		29/12	23/02	19/04	01/09	03/05	01/12	12/01	26/01
Redditch United	03/11	08/09	12/04	08/03	22/03	17/11	09/02	29/03	19/01	22/12	08/12	26/04	18/08	27/08		26/01	22/09	20/10	14/08	05/01	01/01	16/02
Solihull Moors	12/01	23/10	11/08	22/09	20/10	01/09	25/08	15/03	29/12	03/05	19/04	26/12	02/02	08/09	24/03		05/04	01/12	01/03	09/02	08/12	03/11
Southport	25/08	12/01	29/12	17/11	29/03	26/12	11/08	08/12	01/09	06/10	18/09	12/04	26/04	16/02	01/03	15/09		15/03	03/11	27/10	26/01	24/03
Stafford Rangers	19/04	16/02	25/08	08/09	17/11	08/12	23/10	12/01	22/09	03/11	01/01	11/08	27/08	02/02	03/05	29/03	22/12		06/10	12/04	22/03	08/03
Tamworth	26/12	25/08	15/09	19/01	12/04	11/08	20/10	26/04	23/10	16/02	26/01	29/12	01/12	10/11	23/02	05/01	08/03	24/03		29/03	08/09	22/09
Vauxhall Motors	23/10	01/09	26/12	16/02	08/12	29/12	15/03	24/03	19/04	05/04	12/01	01/03	20/10	18/09	11/08	17/11	03/05	15/09	02/02		03/11	25/08
Worcester City	29/12	24/03	01/12	02/02	26/04	01/03	05/04	01/09	05/01	09/02	11/08	25/08	15/09	27/10	26/12	17/09	20/10	10/11	15/03	25/02		19/01
Workington	02/02	26/04	10/11	27/08	23/02	12/01	01/03	27/10	15/03	01/12	22/12	15/09	01/01	18/08	06/10	12/04	14/08	18/09	09/02	22/03	29/03	

95

Football Conference Blue Square South Fixtures 2007/2008	Basingstoke Town	Bath City	Bishop's Stortford	Bognor Regis Town	Braintree Town	Bromley	Cambridge City	Dorchester City	Eastbourne Borough	Eastleigh	Fisher Athletic	Hampton & Richmond	Havant & Waterlooville	Hayes & Yeading United	Lewes	Maidenhead United	Newport County	St. Albans City	Sutton United	Thurrock	Welling United	Weston Super Mare
Basingstoke Town	■	24/03	10/11	12/01	15/03	23/02	25/08	18/09	01/09	01/01	02/02	06/10	16/02	29/03	12/04	03/05	08/12	17/11	11/08	15/09	27/10	22/12
Bath City	20/10	■	17/11	22/12	09/02	19/01	05/04	01/01	03/11	14/08	26/01	18/08	22/03	27/10	08/03	08/12	07/09	22/09	19/04	26/04	16/02	27/08
Bishop's Stortford	05/04	03/05	■	09/02	26/12	15/03	29/12	01/09	02/02	06/10	19/04	18/09	05/01	01/12	27/10	03/11	11/08	07/09	24/03	25/08	19/01	23/02
Bognor Regis Town	29/12	18/09	18/08	■	16/02	05/01	27/10	08/03	07/09	26/01	06/10	14/08	26/12	10/11	27/08	23/02	29/03	12/04	26/04	19/01	01/12	22/03
Braintree Town	03/11	29/03	01/01	17/11	■	14/08	19/01	27/10	03/05	18/08	18/09	22/12	23/02	06/10	12/01	08/09	12/04	27/08	08/03	08/12	22/03	02/02
Bromley	22/09	11/08	15/09	25/08	01/03	■	24/03	03/05	06/10	08/12	29/12	29/03	12/04	01/09	10/11	12/01	17/11	23/10	02/02	26/12	08/03	16/02
Cambridge City	01/03	15/09	27/08	15/03	20/10	22/12	■	16/02	23/10	17/11	12/01	08/12	18/08	26/01	29/03	22/03	26/04	01/01	22/09	10/11	14/08	12/04
Dorchester Town	22/03	26/12	08/12	23/10	26/04	20/10	05/01	■	09/02	27/08	15/09	17/11	14/08	12/04	18/08	15/03	29/12	26/01	23/02	29/03	10/11	22/09
Eastbourne Borough	26/01	12/04	14/08	08/12	15/09	22/03	23/02	22/12	■	12/01	08/03	27/10	27/08	26/04	01/01	18/08	10/11	16/02	20/10	17/11	18/09	29/03
Eastleigh	26/12	05/01	29/03	24/03	01/12	26/04	11/08	02/02	29/12	■	25/08	12/04	10/11	15/03	20/10	01/03	18/09	19/01	01/09	27/10	23/02	08/09
Fisher Athletic	13/08	15/03	22/09	05/04	05/01	27/08	07/09	01/03	01/12	09/02	■	22/03	26/04	16/02	22/12	20/10	27/10	10/11	19/01	12/04	01/01	18/08
Hampton & Richm.	09/02	10/11	23/10	19/04	24/03	26/01	01/09	05/04	11/08	15/09	23/02	■	15/03	29/12	26/04	22/09	25/08	20/10	26/12	12/01	05/01	01/12
Havant & Waterloo.	22/10	06/10	08/03	01/01	11/08	07/09	09/02	12/01	01/03	22/12	17/11	03/11	■	25/08	22/09	19/04	24/03	08/12	05/04	01/09	03/05	26/01
Hayes & Yeading	08/09	01/03	22/03	03/05	05/04	09/02	19/04	19/01	22/09	03/11	23/10	27/08	02/02	■	08/12	01/01	08/03	22/12	17/11	20/10	18/08	14/08
Lewes	05/01	01/12	16/02	02/02	25/08	19/09	06/10	19/04	26/12	05/04	24/03	19/01	29/12	11/08	■	24/10	01/09	15/03	03/11	01/03	07/09	03/05
Maidenhead United	19/01	25/08	12/04	01/09	26/01	27/10	18/09	01/12	05/01	08/03	11/08	16/02	15/09	26/12	09/02	■	06/10	26/04	29/12	24/03	29/03	10/11
Newport County	27/08	24/10	01/03	20/10	22/09	05/04	01/12	03/11	19/04	22/03	03/05	02/02	19/01	05/01	23/02	15/08	■	18/08	15/09	15/03	22/12	01/01
St. Albans City	08/03	23/02	12/01	03/11	29/12	01/12	26/12	11/08	25/08	19/04	01/09	03/05	29/03	24/03	15/09	02/02	09/02	■	05/01	19/09	06/10	27/10
Sutton United	01/12	12/01	22/12	01/03	10/11	18/08	03/05	08/09	15/03	16/02	29/03	01/01	27/10	18/09	22/03	27/08	26/01	14/08	■	09/02	12/04	06/10
Thurrock	18/08	02/02	26/01	22/09	19/04	01/01	08/03	06/10	05/04	03/05	03/11	07/09	01/12	23/02	14/08	22/12	16/02	22/03	23/10	■	27/08	05/01
Welling United	19/04	01/09	26/04	11/08	23/10	03/11	02/02	25/08	24/03	22/09	26/12	01/03	20/10	15/09	26/01	17/11	12/01	05/04	08/12	29/12	■	15/03
Weston-super-Mare	26/04	29/12	20/10	15/09	01/09	19/04	03/11	24/03	19/01	22/10	08/12	08/03	17/09	12/01	17/11	05/04	26/12	01/03	25/08	11/08	09/02	■